Waiting on God

By the same author

Jesus and the Gospels

Jesus and the Gospels:
set of 36 lectures on CD discs

The Parables of Jesus

Seasons of the Word:
Reflections on the Sunday Readings

Impressions of Jesus

The Gospel of Mark

The Gospel of Luke

Emmaus: The Gracious Visit of God
According to Luke

Waiting on God

Becoming What God Wants Us To Be

DENIS McBRIDE

Liguori/Triumph
LIGUORI, MISSOURI

Imprimi Potest:
Richard Thibodeau, C.Ss.R.
Provincial, Denver Province
The Redemptorists

Published by Liguori/Triumph
An imprint of Liguori Publications
Liguori, Missouri
www.liguori.org

Library of Congress Cataloging-in-Publication Data

McBride, Denis.
    Waiting on God : becoming what God wants us to be / Denis McBride.—1st U.S. ed.
        p. cm.
    Includes bibliographical references.
    ISBN 0-7648-1215-7
    1. Christian life—Catholic authors. 2. Spiritual life—Christianity 3. Waiting (Philosophy)—Religious aspects—Christianity. I. Title.

BX2350.3.M326 2004
242—dc22   2004048628

Printed in the United States of America
08 07 06 05 04   5 4 3 2 1
First U.S. Edition 2004

For
my sister Ellen,
a specialist in waiting,
in loving gratitude
for caring for our parents
and for
my Canadian Redemptorist confreres
of the Edmonton-Toronto Province
in grateful recognition
for commissioning these reflections

Contents

Contents

Contents

Chapter One

Waiting: Why Bother?

An Old Priest Waits

When I was invited by some Redemptorists in Canada to offer some biblical reflections on the theme of "Waiting on the Lord," I heard myself instinctively say "Fine" into the phone, as if all my life I had been waiting for someone to invite me to reflect on the subject. When I hung up the phone I sat down in a heap of instant regret. "What have you agreed to?" I asked myself. I looked out my office window at the countless greens of the Shropshire landscape.

The next day I was going to see an old priest that I had met after my ordination. Since then we have remained good friends for thirty years; for me he has been a perceptive guide and a wise mentor. I see him as a collector's item—a wise man from the west—so I thought I'd ask him, my ancient oracle, for some inspiration.

He is an unusual priest, though not unique, because although he is a practicing Catholic he has become an atheist. He stopped believing about ten years ago, yet he is a hugely popular and caring pastor, a man who has time for everyone, especially the sick and homebound. A few years ago he took me into his confidence and told me that he could no longer sign his name to the creed. He said, "My only prayer is that of Mary Magdalene: 'They have taken away my Lord, and I don't know where they have put him.'"

I traveled north to see my atheist-priest. After we exchanged the usual weather reports and medical updates—both a bit bleak,

I have to say—I asked him what he was waiting for. He looked at me, puzzled at a question arriving without any conversational context, and said: "What am I waiting for? I'm waiting for my tea, son."

I said, "Oh, right," and laughed. I thought he might have said the return of the Lord or something, but clearly that could wait. I made him some tea and told him I had to write some reflections on waiting on the Lord for the Redemptorists in Canada; he told me to go for a walk and he would have something for me when I returned.

He doesn't read any newspapers or watch television; he finds the world news not only depressing but predictable, repeating the same stories over and over again as if they have never happened before. His main reading material is poetry, and he keeps a book of psalms and a large collection of poetry beside his armchair. His antiquarian book of the Hebrew psalms is overstuffed with a variety of ancient novenas: to the Infant of Prague, to the Sacred Heart, to Saint Martin de Porres, and to Saint Jude. He still hangs on to these mementos of a lost life, he says, to remind himself of what he once believed. And he has about two hundred volumes of poetry, ancient and modern, which have become his sacred scripture, his word of life. When I returned from my walk he shared with me one of his favorite poems—*Waiting*[1]—written by the Welsh priest-poet, R. S. Thomas.

> Yeats said that. Young
> I delighted in it:
> there was time enough.
>
> Fingers burned, heart
> seared, a bad taste
> in the mouth, I read him
> again, but without trust
> any more. What counsel
> has the pen's rhetoric

to impart? Break mirrors, stare
ghosts in the face, try
walking without crutches

at the grave's edge? Now
in the small hours
of belief the one eloquence

to master is that
of the bowed head, the bent
knee, waiting, as at the end

of a hard winter
for one flower to open
on the mind's tree of thorns.

"I like that," he said. "When you get a bit older, as the poem says, you've had your fingers burned, and your heart seared, and you have a bad taste in your mouth. And the one thing you know is that there is not enough time. No matter how much time you have, even at my age, it's never enough. I've reached the small hours of belief; maybe a flower will still open in this mind of thorns. Who knows? Whatever happens, I realize that at my age the one eloquence to master is waiting."

Waiting is also a theme of a psalm/poem that is particularly well known to Redemptorists:

My soul is waiting for the Lord,
I count on his word.
My soul is longing for the Lord
more than watchman for daybreak.
Let the watchman count on daybreak
and Israel on the Lord.

Because with the Lord there is mercy
and fullness of redemption,
Israel indeed he will redeem
from all its iniquity (Ps 130:5–8).

The motto of the Redemptorist Congregation—*Copiosa apud eum redemptio* ("With him there is plentiful redemption")—is enclosed in this psalm that counsels waiting as a basic spiritual attitude in life. The psalm is a *crie de coeur*, a cry from the depth of the heart for God to pay attention. It is a psalm of longing, a prayer that aches for the Lord more than the night watchman longs to be freed from his dark lookout.

The sentinel faces the lonely boredom of walking back and forth in the dark, where nothing much happens, when the minutes seem like hours, when the dark magnifies every little creak and echoes back every little sound. As the watchman counts on the arrival of the light of dawn, so the psalmist waits hopefully for the Lord. The psalmist is not absorbed with his own discomfort as he struggles to stay awake while everyone else sleeps; rather, he is focused beyond the nighttime. What keeps him going is his conviction that when dawn approaches it will dismiss the dark. The psalmist counts on his belief in who God is—in whom there is *copiosa redemptio*.

The attitude of waiting, however, is not a very popular one in our Western culture. To wait is a countercultural activity. That word culture has shifted in meaning dramatically: it used to refer to literature and music and drama—how we cultivated ourselves—but a new meaning is the dominant one: culture is everything that shapes the human person and the community in which we live. We are shaped by the world we live in: not all of that influence is negative, and some genuine values have come to the fore, like freedom and honesty and a sense of justice.

Work and Identity

One characteristic of our Western culture is the prize we put on work, on achievement, and on career. The worst affliction that can befall you is to be unemployed; for many people, the second worst is when you have to retire. And when people retire, they often feel obliged to say, "Oh, I am busier than ever, you know. Haven't got a minute to spare." The void left by not working must be filled with activities that keep people looking busy. Even in retirement people's dignity seems to be attached to the work ethic; they still have to prove to themselves and others that they are hard at it. It is as if they degrade themselves by answering the question, "What do you do?" by saying, "Not much, really; I wait and let everyone take care of me."

Not so of one of our old priests. Many people reckon that he spent most of his life rehearsing for retirement, so that when he did retire the experience came as no great seismic shift in his life. You would ask him:

"How was your morning?"

"Wonderful," he would say.

"What did you do?"

"Nothing," he would reply, without a rumor of a blush.

An unlikely countercultural figure, he would then shuffle off to do more of what he had been doing all morning. That exchange is disconcerting for those of us who have bought into the belief that work defines who you are. Some of the people who attend our threemonth renewal courses at Hawkstone Hall in England, most of whom have never stopped working during their priestly or religious lives, become nervous at the prospect of "doing nothing for three months." Moving from achieving to receiving, from activity to waiting, from leading to being led—this alarms some people who are afraid of what might emerge in this time of stillness. Some find it difficult to follow the advice, "Be still before the LORD, / and wait patiently for him" (Ps 37:7). Yet we know that God can be known for who God is only when we provide an environment of stillness and quiet.

The Authority of Experience

Other longings, too, have risen to prominence in our culture, among them the desire to escape the daily round of what liturgists call "ordinary time," to shun boredom and delay, and cram the present moment with interesting diversions. Some people commit suicide because they are bored to death: death looks more interesting and holds out more promise than the dull round of what people are pleased to call life.

Everyone knows that time is something that can run out on you. The psalmist wanted to taste and see that the Lord was good, but our culture hungers to taste and see whatever life has to offer. In our culture what can be is tasted and tested by experience. "Try it," the advice goes, "and if it feels good, it's all right."

I think it is true to say that since the 1960s, experience has gained a new authority in people's thinking: more and more people are becoming their own center of moral authority, rather than objective codes or laws; people are using their own experience as a guiding source of wisdom. Experience means learning through direct personal contact with people and things. New experiences, of course, can challenge us to think again. Many people are moving away from an automatic respect for authority and authority figures to an instinctive respect for their own experience and judgment. That is a dramatic shift. Authority, whether political or religious, much more than before, has to earn the respect of people before it is acknowledged and heeded.

Time magazine in its cover story—"Where Did God Go? A Special Report on Christianity in Europe"—compiled from fifteen of its reporters across Europe, comments:

Both at the national and individual levels, religion is going private. Churches across Europe are boarding up—or being turned into pubs, homes, even supermarkets. Citizens, like states, are rethinking their relationship with clergy and fashioning their own relationship with God. Says Ján Suchán, a Catholic priest in Slovakia who hosts a popular radio show: "The more independent people become, the less they need someone to lead them by the hand." French orthodox theologian Olivier Clément terms this a "quest for liberty of the spirit." He predicts that "at the end of this path will open a new age of Christianity."[2]

In the light of exposures in the media of clerical exploitation, the church has seen the power of its authority and traditional influence diminish significantly: the view of a growing number of people is that the church has to regain people's confidence as a moral guide. There is a crisis of credibility. Although there have been no challenges to Gospel teaching or revealed dogmas, many practicing Catholics simply ignore whole sections of the Church's moral teaching that do not square with their own experience. Father Donald Cozzens has analyzed these changes well in his writings.[3] Even in popular novels, the portrait of the priest is often someone who is out of kilter with the collective discernment of ordinary folk. For example, in the popular novel, *The Dead of Winter*, the character Pierre Rousseau says of his brother, who is a priest:

I have to remind myself that Jerome is not a bad man, that he means well. Yet he suffers from institutional deformation. He has spent so much time in schools and seminaries that his vision of evil is askew. Wars, exploitation, political terror are not in his purview. Instead, he has a heightened sensitivity to sex, to rebellion against authority, to pride. He is as alert to these homely transgressions as a medieval inquisitor.[4]

Countering the Church's traditional moral teaching, and its priests, with the discernment of what people actually believe and how they behave is a new growth industry. The growing respect for experience, which has affected Catholics as it has most social groupings, has resulted in an increasing tolerance of ambiguity to embrace the vast differences in people's preferences and lifestyles. Women, gays, ethnic and religious minorities, for example, are coming out of isolation, coming together, and finding a common voice to protest against the oppression they have suffered. They are no longer going to suffer in silence. Their experience, they declare, counts. They want to register their hurt and their right to be themselves. Who they are matters. So they tell their stories, and often this story of distress makes its own compelling argument and sometimes has the moral force to lead others to change their minds. As the Dutch theologian E. Schillebeeckx has noted:

> Anyone who has had an experience *ipso facto* becomes himself a witness: he has a message. He describes what has happened to him. This narration opens up a new possibility of life for others, it sets something in motion. Thus the authority of experience becomes operative in the telling. The authority of experience has a narrative structure.[5]

Through television and films, through books and magazines, our Western culture has become a culture of storytelling—not the legends and myths and sagas of the past, but the dramas of ordinary people whose experience has its own distinctive power and authority. Apart from soap operas, so much television has become the "fly on the wall" variety—like "Big Brother" or "Survivors"—observing and recording how people manage to live together in community, to relate to one another, or survive one another. Living in the absence of community themselves, many people tune in to television to find a fictional substitute.

The old manuals of moral theology used the phrase *experientia docet*—experience teaches—to make the point that experience itself is our teacher. That still holds good. The power of experience is demonstrated by a successful book which looks at how men and women differ—John Gray's *Men Are From Mars, Women Are From Venus*. It was a publisher's dream, secure in the bestseller list for more than a decade. The success of the book is that it stays within the orbit of human experience, gathering its wisdom from the experience of twenty-five thousand men and women in relationship seminars. It analyzes how men and women radically differ, explores these human differences, and uncovers new ways of improving relationships. It appeals only to human experience. As the author notes, "The truth of these principles is self-evident and can be validated by your own experience as well as by common sense."[6]

The Culture of Immediacy

Not only has experience gained a new authority in our social order, but, alongside that, we have become a culture of immediacy, a culture hungry for instant results and the quick fix, a people whose desire for the new has to be transformed into the present tense. We want it now. Why wait when you can get it now? The world of advertising is a world of voices and images soliciting and insisting that *what we want is what we need* and all of it can be purchased now.

We are the generation of the present moment: if it isn't happening now, it's no good. There is little tolerance for things that don't work, not least relationships. We dispose effortlessly not only of gadgets that no longer work or are outdated, but of relationships that seem worn out, where there is no longer any payoff.

Many young people are cautious about entering a lifelong relationship and solemnly promising each other, before an assembly of witnesses, that forever is their timetable; they are wary about committing themselves to each other "till death do us part." This is understandable when they see the breakdown of so many marriages. Some think it wiser to tiptoe into marriage with a trial relationship, when everything can be experienced now, except living inside the promise of lifelong fidelity. The singer Rod Stewart has suggested that marriage vows should be made for three years; for him, that is the span of eternity and the extent modern people can reasonably be expected to commit themselves to each other.

People have grown accustomed to immediate gratification: why wait? And often when we get what we want, trying it out or buying it in the hope we will be satisfied at last, the vacancy is not filled. That experience of dissatisfaction is often characteristic of our world of consumerism. As one observer noted sharply:

> Last Christmas I sat in a café inside a fashionable department store, watching the shoppers come and go. Most of them, I thought, had come not to buy things they already wanted. It was as if they had come looking for something to want—something that might fill a nameless need, even if only for a moment.[7]

So the hunt goes on for something that will satisfy the huge hunger inside us. Our hunger for the immediate is insatiable. The faster the better. We have fast foods, microwaves, faxes, mobile phones, computers, and the Internet. We want to download the world immediately, to have everything instantly available. When I was preparing these reflections I logged onto the Internet, clicked on the Google browser and typed in the word waiting. The browser informed me that over 7,110,000 articles were available instantly in cyberspace—which made the task utterly impossible. Paradoxically, I gave up under the sheer weight of what was available. Sometimes having everything accessible creates its own problems.

For many people, waiting is regarded as a waste of time, it is the empty landscape between where we are and where we want to be, between what we don't have and what we desire. It is the place where nothing happens. This is symbolized in the doctor's waiting room: whatever is happening is happening somewhere else, not here; here is a place where time seems to stand still, where time is put on hold, where time comes to a crunching halt.

In our society there is a direct correlation between status and waiting. The more important your status, the less you have to wait. Waiting reminds us that we are not in charge, that we cannot command instantly whatever it is we seek, so we have to wait. And the people who always have to wait are the poor.

As one old African-American woman told me when I was studying in the Bronx in New York: "Look at this place for God's sake! Look! The future never happens here. The future always happens somewhere else." For her, the neighborhood was not a place for waiting in hope but a rubbish heap doomed to remain eternally unchanged. There seems little point in waiting for yesterday.

Having to wait, in traffic jams, at supermarket checkouts, and at hospitals and airports, these places have become "hot spots" for anger in a rising tide of impatience. According to Ellis Cashmore, who lectures in culture and media at Staffordshire University, rage will become the defining emotion of the twenty-first century unless action is taken to reduce people's growing lack of tolerance to waiting. In an interview he observed:

> Some areas of life have failed to keep pace with the rapid development of technology and communication. All involve waiting. We have grown impatient because we have become accustomed to getting what we want instantly in so many other areas of life. We are becoming less tolerant in delays in gratification. We just can't

speed up some parts of life as we can others, so we need to think creatively how to distract people, to take their minds off the waiting so they do not grow impatient. In Disney World the organizers tackled the problem of frustrated customers in huge queues for popular rides by sending out workers dressed as Mickey and Goofy to joke with the waiting customers and have photographs taken with them.[8]

The professor is a child, not a critic of the time. He sees the present task not to promote serenity or patience, but to distract people from the pain of waiting, to fool them with diversions, to give them the impression *something* is happening. We are now being asked to do what, in the language of the old confessional, we admitted somewhat timidly: that we entertained distractions. Now we have to find the equivalent of Mickey Mouse to quiet an impatient and frustrated world.

Waiting to Be Avoided

There are occasions in life, of course, when the last thing to do is wait, when not acting can put others in danger and can sometimes cost lives. Sometimes urgent action is what is needed and "waiting on God" becomes a feat of magical belief rather than an act of faith. The best example I could find is in a newspaper report, taken from *The Salt Lake City Tribune*, of a man who waited nine weeks for God's intervention while his pickup was stuck in a snowdrift. The report, see text box, speaks for itself.

Fatal Faith: Snowbound Driver Dies
Waiting for God to Save Him

The Salt Lake City Tribune, June 3, 1995
Jeff Barnard, The Associated Press

AGNESS, ORE. — When DeWitt Finley got stuck in the snow last fall trying to drive the back roads over the Klamath Mountains, he put his faith in God and waited with the patience of Job for someone to rescue him. For nine weeks, he sat in his pickup, checked the days off the calendar in his day planner and wrote a stack of letters in a neat hand on a legal pad to his two sons, his fiancée and his boss. If only he had stepped out of the truck and followed the road back along a corner, he soon would have found clear pavement leading him down the mountain to safety.

Last month, after some teenagers who got stuck themselves discovered Finley starved to death in his truck, the people who live in this rugged country could not believe he had just sat there for so long.

The snow "never stays on this road but right there," said Glenn Carpenter of Gold Beach, who dug Finley's pickup out of five feet of snow with a front-end loader on May 22 before going on to open the road for the season. Depending on the weather, Finley could have had a few hundred yards or a few miles of snow to walk through before reaching pavement, Carpenter said. But there is no sign he ever had left his truck.

"I have no control over my life. It's all in His hands. 'His will be done,'" Finley wrote his boss in one of the letters found with his body. "Death here in another month or so, or he sends someone to save me. Yet knowing His will I'm at peace and His grace will prevail. If I'm saved to finish my life here, please know I'll always

be thankful to you and remain your servant. If not—
I'll see you in Glory."

Sheriff's Detective Allen Boice figures that Finley, having spent most of his life in California, was in unfamiliar circumstances.

Finley, fifty-six, was on a sales trip through Oregon, hauling a brand-new demo camper on the back of a four-wheel-drive diesel pickup, when he decided November 14 to leave the main highway along the coast to take the back roads through the Siskiyou National Forest to Grants Pass.

The Bear Camp Road has lots of traffic in the summer, when whitewater rafters on the Rogue River use it to shuttle their rigs from Galice to Agness. But when the snow comes, the Forest Service does not plow it. The day after Finley drove up, rangers posted a sign at the bottom reading: "Road may be blocked by snowdrifts six miles ahead."

Tow-truck driver Everett Amos gets calls to haul out people each winter. Sometimes they call on a cellular phone or a CB radio. Finley had neither. Otherwise they walk out, like the teenagers who found Finley on May 20. It is sixteen miles down the mountain, and one more mile to the Cougar Lane Store.

After Finley vanished, his boss, Mic Sieler, owner of S & S Campers, sent out another man to search for him. Deputies in Coos Bay, his last stop, sent up a helicopter.

Meanwhile, Finley accepted his fate, writing calmly to Sieler. "Typical Oregon weather, clear for a few days and storms for the next few days, has left me in a tomb for the past thirty days," Finley wrote.

"The most wonderful thing out of this ordeal has been the neverending fellowship with the Lord. I've not eaten since noon of November 14 yet I feel great and I'm in good spirits. I've never known such fellowship nor how His plan for man can be a love for us beyond all things."

Finley kept crossing off the days on his calendar until January 19.

"It was a senseless death," said Jim Kelley of the Forest Service. "That's what's so sad about it."

Finley kept the faith, but lost his life.

The protagonist in the story, Mr. Finley, was not condemned by fate to die, nor was he powerless to act; there were options open to him that he could have taken to save his own life, just as the teenagers did in the same situation. For him to write, "I have no control over my life," was simply untrue: he could have walked away from his tomb by himself; instead, he chose to stay, a decision that cost him his life. Passive acceptance of an imagined fate is not the same as waiting on God: those who wait on God wait inside the dynamic of God's promise because they are powerless to bring about what they hope for; those who passively accept their imagined fate wait inside their elected immobility.

There are examples in the Gospels where action rather than waiting is exemplified as the proper response. A few examples will suffice:

- ❖ Jesus does not wait until the Sabbath is over before curing people.
- ❖ He rejects his disciples' advice to dismiss the hungry crowd and challenges them to action, "Give them something to eat" (Mk 6:37).
- ❖ Jesus offers his disciples an energetic model in the host who receives a visitor at midnight and goes off immediately to hunt for bread (Lk 11:5–8).
- ❖ He counsels his disciples to be "dressed for action" (Lk 12:35).

❖ Jesus curses the fig tree for its fruitlessness (Mt 21:8–21).

❖ Jesus tells the chief priests: "The kingdom of God will be taken from you and given to a people that produces fruits to the kingdom" (Mt 21:43).

❖ On discovering their losses, two characters act immediately: the shepherd seeks out the lost sheep while the woman searches for her lost coins (Lk 15:1–10).

❖ The crafty steward is praised because he is galvanized into immediate action by his dismissal (Lk 16:1–8).

❖ The widow is held up to the disciples as a model of action because she badgers the judge unremittingly until he dispenses justice (Lk 18:1–8).

❖ The blind man refuses the crowd's counsel to stay quiet and remain as he is; instead, he energetically screams to Jesus for help (Lk 18:35–43).

If there is a time and season for everything, there is time for action and a time for waiting, a time to take charge of a situation and a time to recognize one's own inability to make any difference.

Waiting Not to Be Avoided

We know that there *are* experiences in life when waiting cannot be avoided, when the business of living is the business of waiting. We can all call to mind our own images of waiting.

❖ A woman stands at the end of a pier, her eyes scanning the horizon as she waits for her husband's ship to come home.

❖ An ancient father climbs a hill to his lookout in the tenacious hope that his younger son will one day come home. In the meantime, all he can do is wait.

❖ Young parents wait with growing expectation for the birth of their child.

❖ An old man sits in a nursing home, still waiting for the day when his family will visit him.

All wait for something new to happen; all wait for a happy ending they cannot write, for a "not yet" that sometimes might feel like a "not ever." And that waiting tests the quality of their hope. They are powerless to bring about what they hope for; that is why they wait.

We know from our own experience that waiting is part of life, and there is no life without it. All of us waited to be born, we waited to be nourished, we waited to be named, and we waited to be loved.

Love and waiting are very close. You say to someone, "I love you." Then you have to wait. After you make your risky speech, you have to stop, wait, and listen for the response. And if you are greeted with a puzzled silence, you can go quietly nuts inside your head. The other person might say: "Big deal, so what? Who cares?" And then you go totally loopy. Whatever happens, you cannot manage the response or write the script: you have to bide your time for the reply, wait in the silence that follows your affirmation. Love is only love when there is a free response.

In Roland Barthes' wonderful book, *A Lover's Discourse*, he writes:

> "Am I in love?—Yes, since I am waiting." The other never waits. Sometimes I want to play the part of the one who doesn't wait; I try to busy my life elsewhere, to arrive late; but I always lose at this game: whatever I do, I find myself there, with nothing to do, punctual, even ahead of time. The lover's fatal identity is precisely: *I am the one who waits.*
>
> A mandarin fell in love with a courtesan. "I shall be

yours," she told him, "when you have spent a hundred nights waiting for me, sitting on a stool, in my garden, beneath my windows." But on the ninety-ninth night, the mandarin stood up, put his stool under his arm, and went away."[9]

Barthes' mandarin is no longer in love: we know that because he has no time anymore; he has stopped waiting. Lovers always wait. In Barthes' phrase, it is their fatal identity. Divorce is the decision to stop waiting together: two people who were in love once upon a time have now run out of patience; they have literally no time for each other anymore. They no longer wait on each other or wait together. The most common accusation of the hurt lover is the refrain: "You have no time for me."

The same is true of family life or religious community. One of the signs of lack of love in family and community is when we have no time for one another, when we never spend time together or wait together. We can become people who are always on the way somewhere else. People are rushing off, heading elsewhere, hurrying to commitments, to appointments, to fulfillment—to something over there. Over there is where it is all happening, not here. They greet you on their way out, as they head for the door, car keys jangling, their eyes hungry for the exit. Sometimes the older members of our family or community must wonder why everything is happening out there and not here, at home.

Yet most of us opt for family or community life because we choose to live and work together, rather than alone; to wait together, rather than wait alone. We believe that in community something is happening *here*, among us, in the present. We live together, we pray together, we eat together, we share together the fortunes and misfortunes of our life.

Gertrud Nelson makes an interesting suggestion when she writes:

Pre-Christian peoples who lived far north and who suffered the loss of life and light with the disappearance of the sun had a way of wooing back life and hope. Their solution was to bring all ordinary action and daily routine to a halt. They gave into the nature of winter, came away from the fields. And put away their tools. They removed the wheels from their carts and wagons, festooned them with greens and lights and brought them in to hang on their halls. They brought the wheels indoors as a sign of a different time, a time to stop and turn inward. Slowly, slowly they wooed the sun god back.

That kind of success can only be accomplished when we have had the courage to stop and wait and engage fully in the winter of our dark longing. Perhaps the symbolic energy of those wheels made sacred has escaped us when we wish to relegate our Advent wreaths to the realms of quaint custom or pretty decorations.

Imagine what would happen if we were to understand that ancient prescription literally and remove— just one—say the right front tire from our cars and use this for our Advent wreath. Indeed, things would stop. Having to stay put, we would lose the opportunity to escape or deny our feelings or becomings because our cars could not bring us away to the circus in town.[10]

But who would risk following that advice? What would we do together? How would we pass the time? Perhaps we have lost the art of being together without a task to focus on, without an agenda to plow through, without business to transact. Being present to one another, wasting time together in shared space, makes many of us uneasy and fidgety as we long for the solitary space of our rooms and gadgets. For many people living in family or community, the practice of waiting together around a common hearth, rather than being alone in one's room, has become an unlamented memory of the way things were. Perhaps the communal hearth has gone; perhaps central heating in every room has displaced communality.

Chapter Two

Waiting for God

The King and the Runners

Once upon a time there was a king who ruled over an untroubled land, a land so peaceful that the only thing the people worried about was who would succeed the king. This worried the king as well. He had prayed to all the gods in turn, begging them for a son and heir, and spent years waiting for a reply. All the gods remained silent, but at last one spoke to the king as his sixty-eighth year was coming to a close, in the third watch of the night. Chronos, the god of time, spoke to the king in a vision and told him that there would be no annunciation of the birth of his son because he would die childless. He would have to choose one of his own people to succeed him.

The king waited a little longer, in case there was another word, but he gradually came to accept the truth that he would die without an heir, and that his remaining time would be best spent in choosing a suitable successor. He announced to his people that he would choose an heir to the throne from among the young men of the country by a competitive test that would give all an equal chance. The heralds announced this throughout the land and, of course, there were as many applicants as there were young men.

The king put all the aspirants though a series of trials: there were tests for intellectual strength, for physical prowess, for spiritual insight, and for the virtues of leadership. The number was whittled down to fifty. After another range of tests the number was reduced to three. One of these three would be the new king. The old king, who was now threescore years and ten, devised other tests. The three were put through test after test, but all seemed equally able to meet them, so the king announced that on the next day the matter would be decided finally by a race.

The course was marked off, the judges were at their places, and all was ready. Just before the race one of the king's counselors approached each of the contestants in turn and said secretly to each one, "The king is taking special note of you. Do not run when the signal is given; run only when the king gives you a special signal." The three took their places, eager for the race.

The chief judge gave the signal for the race to begin, and one runner bounded forward immediately, then hesitated and stopped; then another sprang forward after him; the first started forward again and the two of them ran for the goal with all speed. The third stood looking anxiously at the king and at the two runners, murmuring to himself, "I can still make it, I can still make it." The king gazed at the runners and paid no attention to the one still standing. The third man thought he had been forgotten and soon realized that it would be impossible for him to win the race.

The two runners ran on at top speed, reaching the goal together. They were brought back, and all three stood before the king. To the first he said, "You were told not to run until I gave you the signal. Why then did you run?"

"I was so excited about winning that I forgot," said the man.

He asked the same question of the second runner. He replied, "When I saw the other man running, I thought he had received the special signal from you, so I ran as well."

To the third he said, "And why did you not run?"

"Because your majesty did not give me the signal," he answered.

"I knew that you could run," said the king, "but I did not know that you could wait. The test was not about running; it was about waiting, for I have waited all my life for this day, my son."

> The LORD is good to those who wait for him,
> to the soul that seeks him.
> It is good that one should wait quietly
> for the salvation of the LORD (Lam 3:25–26).

Abraham and Sarah: Waiting for New Life

The ancient story of our faith begins with two great figures of waiting, Abraham and Sarah, celebrated as the ancestors of the Jews, the Christians and the Muslims. The international magazine *Time* celebrated Abraham on their cover with an accompanying report, reflecting on whether this celebrated founding figure, respected by three great faiths, might still function as a peacemaker among them.[1]

In the *Koran* Abraham is known as *El Khalil*, the friend of God. Hebron, the place where Abraham and Sarah are buried—still one of the hot spots of Israeli-Palestinian fighting—is called *El Khalil* by the Palestinians. The Jaffa Gate in the old city of Jerusalem, which marks the beginning of the road to Hebron, is inscribed with a verse from the Koran: "There is no god but Allah and Abraham is his friend."

Abraham and Sarah are the most ecumenical figures in the history of religion—they are wanted and claimed by three major faiths. These two old people are God's original accomplices. At a time when people the same age are already well retired, Abraham and Sarah begin a new life by leaving their own place and country for a great adventure. They leave their settled town life and become nomads, without a clue where they are going. Their only fixed point is in their heart, their belief in the promise of God. This elderly couple are the original pilgrims, our ancestors in the faith. The story of our faith begins with two old gypsies who set out on a journey without maps, traveling on a word of promise.

The Israelites called him "our father Abraham"—because he was a father not only of a family, but a people. His story begins with a word of promise:

> I will make of you a great nation, and I will bless you, and make your name great so that you will be a blessing. I will bless those who bless you, and the one who curses I will curse; and in you all the families of the earth shall be blessed (Gen 12:3).

When Abraham is called he is seventy-five years old. He is already a veteran, a man who is chronologically advantaged over the rest of his tribe. Sarah is ten years younger, a healthy sixty-five-year-old, a beauty who still attracts the attention of pharaohs and sheiks. But she is long past childbearing age and has been afflicted with barrenness all her life. As a couple they share an impressive arithmetic of years *and* an impressive handicap: they have no need to go to the local doctor and ask why nothing is happening in the baby department; they do not need prophets to explain the empty crib.

God promises these two antiques that they will be a new beginning, a fresh start, and become ancestors to peoples whose number will be as countless as the stars. That is the promise. You can imagine the two old flames looking up at the night sky filled with stars, then looking at each other differently, wondering if this is all a cruel joke, unsure if they should put their walking sticks in storage. But they both believe the word of promise; they make it their daily bread, in spite of all signs to the contrary. They eat the promise, they savor it, and they are nourished by it. And they know well that they can do nothing about it: all they can do is wait. And it takes another twenty-five years before that promise is fulfilled.

Abraham and the patriarchs were men who were not settled in one place or country; rather, they lived in tents and moved from one location to another. They were not farmers but shepherds, not settlers but pioneers; they were bedouins, nomadic spirits who were often referred to as "strangers" in the land. The gods of settled inhabitants are generally linked to particular sacred places, fixed sanctuaries, where people go to worship. This is unworkable for a nomadic group; their god is not a god of place but the god who spoke to their ancestors, a god of the community. God's sacred word, not a sacred place, is the focus of their religious lives.

By the time Abraham is eighty-five years old, he has waited ten long years for a son; he and Sarah are not getting any younger, and the prospects are diminishing by the hour. They are exhausted with waiting: they begin to suspect that the "not yet" really means "not ever." So they decide to take things into their own hands and move to Plan B, to arrange the birth of a son by hiring a host mother. Sarah suggests that Abraham sleep with her Egyptian slave, Hagar. The old patriarch has another look at Hagar and readily agrees.

Why should they bother living in this endless wilderness of waiting when Hagar can provide a son now? Why bother holding out for God's promise when you can arrange what you yearn for yourself? To avoid all the waiting, they go for the quick fix. They want to make life happen, not let life happen; they want to manage it all themselves because they are tired of living this inbetween life, in no man's land, between the promise and the delivery.

Although Hagar conceives the child that Sarah so desperately wants, the arrangement doesn't work. The quick fix threatens to break up the family. With her new authority, the slave girl mocks her barren mistress whom she hopes to replace. Sarah then complains to Abraham: "I count for nothing in your eyes" (Gen 16:5). Because Sarah believes she is of no account, she then mistreats Hagar so badly that the girl runs away. As a privileged woman, Sarah is happy to exploit the fertility of her slave, but she cannot abide Hagar's contempt.

The family that was once united in waiting together in hope has become dysfunctional, suspicious, jealous, and fearful. Both women become victim and victimizer. Later, an annunciation is made to Hagar, now a runaway in the wilderness, about her son: "A wild ass of man he will be...setting himself to defy his brothers" (Gen 16:12). The angel tells Hagar to name her son Ishmael and to return to the family, which she does. She gives a son to Abraham, now in his eighty-sixth year. Plan B looks hopeful, for at last the old couple have a long-awaited son, even if it is arranged outside the promise of God. Eleven years on from God's original promise, if they look objectively at the prospects of Plan A, for all the divine sanction, that plan looks doomed.

Promises and Expectations

When events in our life are not going according to plan, when our hope seems wrecked, we all share our doom-laden outlook with others. We can look at our prospects as a family or religious community and end up sharing only our disappointment and misery. Nearly always someone will voice the bleak annunciation: "Oh, you think things are bad now, but, believe me, they will get much worse." We can give our fiat to this news, nodding readily in agreement. Soon all we do is gather together to concelebrate in hopelessness. But the word of God always comes to contradict hopelessness: that is why it is called Good News. It takes us beyond the boundaries of our own limitation and challenges us to face the future in the power of God's word.

Vaclav Havel, former president of the Czech Republic and a political prisoner for years, was asked in an interview: "Do you see a grain of hope anywhere?" He replied:

> I should probably say first that the kind of hope I often think about (especially in situations that are particu-

larly hopeless, such as prison) I understand above all as a state of mind, not a state of the world. Either we have hope within us or we don't; it is a dimension of the soul, *and it's not essentially depend*ent on some particular observation of the world or estimate of the situation.

Hope is not prognostication. It is an orientation of the spirit, an orientation of the heart; it transcends the world that is immediately experienced, and is anchored somewhere beyond its horizons.

I think the deepest and most important form of hope, the only one that can keep us above the water, and the only true source of the breathtaking dimension of the human spirit and its efforts, is something we get, as it were, from "elsewhere."[2]

That observation is a profound one: hope is not essentially dependent on some particular observation of the world or estimate of the situation. Hope is not prognostication; prognosis means literally "to know before," like a doctor who forecasts a patient's future in the light of the symptoms he sees. Prognostication is based on the evidence; hope comes from elsewhere. A doctor's prognosis of Abraham and Sarah would be fairly predictable; he could scribble nothing on a prescription to help them. Even Viagra would be useless.

Abraham and Sarah catch their hope from elsewhere, not from an estimate of their medical condition. Their hope is founded on a word of promise that comes from the elsewhere that is God. As they count on the word, the word accounts for why they wait.

My soul is waiting for the Lord,
I count on his word (Ps 130:5).

The word addressed to them is in the form of a promise. But none of us can have faith in a promise unless we can see that *what* is promised is a real possibility for ourselves. We must believe that the content of the promise has our name written on it; we must claim the promise for ourselves, holding it close to our hearts, allowing it to form our lives. Believing in promises shapes the way we look at ourselves and the way we look at the future.

Promises must meet expectations. As the sayings go: "When people expect nothing, nothing happens"; "He who expects nothing will not be disappointed." If we have no expectations, promises will bypass us as words heading elsewhere, routed for someone else's address. By their nature promises speak of events yet unfulfilled; they refer us to a future of accomplishment and invite us to wait in hope. If you never risk hoping, you never need wait.

If we are to believe the promises of God, we have to imagine ourselves differently, to see ourselves in a new light. So much of our failure is a failure of imagination: we cannot imagine ourselves differently. We can get stuck with who we are and what we are and where we are. We can become transfixed by the present muddle, expecting nothing more exciting than the same kind of time being endlessly repeated. We can stay hugging the familiar shores of our little lake of Galilee, *per omnia saecula saeculorum*. The word of God invites us to go out into the deep, into the deep of promise.

Some people counter the word of promise with their litany of disappointment and regret:

> Ah,
> if only I was younger,
> if only I was more intelligent,
> if only I was in better health,
> if only I was in a better mood,
> if only...

Some people cancel the future of promise because they don't believe anything will be really different. But there are no facts about the future except one: the only sure thing about the future is that we will die. The rest is open. The future is open, no matter what age we are, no matter what condition or shape we are in—a truth dramatically illustrated by Abraham and Sarah.

Failure to Imagine God's Promise

When Abraham is ninety-nine, knocking on the door of a century, he hears the promise again: "As for Sarah, your wife, I will bless her and give you a son by her: kings and nations will come from her" (Gen 17:15–16). The old patriarch's response is sharply observed in the text. He bows to the ground before God, and when he is down there he has a good laugh to himself, trying to envisage in his mind's eye old Sarah having a child *now at ninety* with himself as the unlikely father. He can no longer imagine this. Sarah's name in Hebrew means "princess"— ninety-yearold princesses are way beyond the promise of their name. Abraham's name means "father of a multitude"—which now seems a dreadful irony.

After twenty-four years of waiting, it is all too much; it is absurd theater, unreal. Muted despair threatens to take over from hope. Bowed to the ground, Abraham can see only what everyone else sees when they look at both of them: not the prince and princess, but an obsolete couple whose future is well behind them. Abraham laughs at the sheer silliness of it all. So when he straightens himself up again, he asks for Ishmael to be recognized as his son: "Oh, let Ishmael live in your presence" (Gen 17:18).

Abraham does not ask that God's old promise be brought into the present tense, but only for the recognition of what he and Sarah and Hagar have managed to accomplish on their own initiative. Why can't God just recognize Ishmael as the rightful heir? Why can't God bless what has happened rather than insisting on this dream that is long overdue? Abraham speaks honestly. Like Edgar in Shakespeare's King Lear who stammers the curtain down on tragedy as he says:

> The weight of this sad time we must obey
> Speak what we feel, not what we ought to say.[3]

Abraham speaks out of the profound sadness he is feeling. I find this particular scene in Genesis very moving. It is frighteningly real. It is easy to see the old man, as we can see ourselves, doubled up in laughter at the sheer farce our life has become, a laughter that is as much self-abusive as it is mocking. Because Abraham fails to imagine Sarah and himself as real parents, the waiting and the hoping seem a vacant pastime. It is not only that they are asked to believe in the birth of their son, they are to imagine themselves differently as parents of this new life. As the writing makes clear, Abraham's failure is a failure of imagination: he wants to settle for what he knows, for what is present, for the here and now, not for a future he cannot imagine anymore.

Abraham expresses his wish that Ishmael be accepted. He already is the parent of Ishmael; at least Ishmael is here, whereas the promised son is still nowhere around. But God refuses the old man, insisting that Sarah will have a son.

Earlier Abraham had been asked to look up at the night sky, and count the stars (Gen 15:6). His descendants, he was told, would be as numberless as the stars in the heavens. Back then, Abraham had believed that the night sky held the secret to his future; but now he looks no longer at the night sky in awesome wonder; he no longer looks up, but, bowed down, looks closer to home, at himself and his wife, at their utter vulnerability.

And he sees not a vision, but a joke—which is why he laughs. He sees two wretched old people who, once upon a time, used to dream of counting the stars as if they were totaling up the multitude of their offspring. Abraham becomes fixated with what is; he has stopped dreaming of what can be; he becomes obsessed with his own poverty, his own emptiness, and, above all, the huge absence that dominates his life. That is why he asks God to settle for the makeshift present, not the future of dreams.

Abraham and Sarah seem not unlike the two tramps in Samuel Beckett's astonishing play, *Waiting for Godot*. The two tramps are homeless, old, and weary, and they spend their time waiting for this character Godot to turn up, waiting for this miracle to happen. The audience only has to glance at the program to know that Mr. Godot will never appear. The subject of the play is how to wait and pass the time, given that the situation is hopeless. The play never really develops from the opening two lines:

Estragon: Nothing to be done.
Vladimir: I'm beginning to come around to that opinion.[4]

Abraham and Sarah have already waited a quarter of a century for a son of their own. Is there nothing to be done? Waiting for that son of promise seems a fruitless enterprise. But God placates the old man by taking account of his concern for Ishmael, promising that he shall indeed bless Ishmael and make him fruitful. More importantly, God insists that he will establish his covenant with Isaac, whom Sarah shall bear next year (Gen 17:21).

The future will be fulfilled according to the promise of God, not the planning of the old couple. The patriarch wants to control what remains of the future, but he has to wait on a future that will happen according to God's word, not his own wishes. And that is difficult. Against the odds, Abraham and Sarah are asked to believe that there really is a way. Sarah is asked to look beyond the tangle of their arrangements to a hidden plan that will be revealed. Like the woman in Adrienne Rich's poem, *The Parting: II,*[5]

White morning flows into the mirror.
Her eye, still old with sleep,
meets itself like a sister.

How they slept last night,
the dream that caged them back to back,
was nothing new.

Last words, tears, most often
come wrapped as the everyday
familiar failure.

Now pulling the comb slowly
through her loosened hair
she tries to find the parting;

it must come out after all:
hidden in all that tangle
there is a way.

Learning to Dream Again

There is a way. The good news is that Abraham and Sarah learn
to dream again, for this time the annunciation specifies a time:
it will happen next year. Honestly. No kidding. That timing
gives substance to their battered hope; it brings them back into
the arena of waiting. So, you watch this old couple learn again
the stubborn habit of hoping; you watch them strain beyond
their own disenchantment to reclaim what they were beginning
to lose. You watch them as they wearily say, "Here we go again."

Paradoxically, the dream that God holds out to them is more
real than what they see, because it is the dream that holds the
truth, not what they behold. Sometimes it is our dreams that tell
us who we are, not our reading of reality. Sometimes it is our
perception of reality that is flawed, not our hopes. Our dreams
and our hopes can be the most real thing about us. If the way we
see things holds no openness to the future, no surprise, then we

have become a closed book, where the ending is already written. That is hell, the place where nothing changes. In the dreams, we dream we entertain strangeness, difference, new possibility. Our waking dreams keep us alert and give us a sense of purpose.

As T. E. Lawrence, better known as Lawrence of Arabia, noted in *The Seven Pillars of Wisdom*:

> All people dream, but not equally. Those who dream by night in the dusty recesses of their minds wake in the day to find it was vanity. But the dreamers of the day are dangerous people, for they may act on their dreams with open eyes to make it possible.

Abraham and Sarah learn to nurture their waking dream again. At the Oak of Mamre three mysterious visitors arrive and the pledge to Abraham is confirmed. After Sarah serves her guests, she is expected to disappear like the good wife and leave the serious men to deliberate among themselves; but she hangs around with a hungry ear, listening at the entrance of the tent. And when she hears the news that she will certainly give birth to a child within a year she starts to laugh and laugh.

You watch her. There she is, this old crone, bent double, her bones creaking, laughing through her false teeth that the wilderness inside her will become a garden. You watch her shake and wheeze as the tears run down her face. You wonder if she is cracking up. She laughs at the idea that a child will be born not in the maternity ward but the geriatric ward. Sarah laughs; and this laughter is the laughter of liberation, not self-mockery, the laughter of relief after all this waiting. She laughs so much that she gives herself away; her laughter brings her out of her hiding place. Sarah gets the joke, for this is comedy. And when God says, "You laughed"—she hastily denies it; to admit the laughter is to admit she was snooping.

Tragedy is what many people expect in life. If tragedy is suffering the inevitable, comedy is celebrating the unexpected, the laughter that salutes what we did not really anticipate. And when their son is born, they name him Isaac—which in Hebrew has its root meaning in laughter.

The story of salvation moves from tragedy to comedy. In his reflections on the history of ideas in the theater, Walter Kerr, formerly the distinguished theater critic of *The New York Times*, writes about the tragic source of comedy:

> Comedy, it seems, is never the gaiety of things; it is the groan made gay. Laughter is not man's first impulse; he cries first. Comedy always comes second, late, after the fact and in spite of it or because of it....
>
> We have very good evidence to show that comedy, in its fullness, comes after seriousness, after tragedy or its equivalent. And, on somewhat lesser but nonetheless extremely provocative evidence, it seems likely that comedy comes from tragedy.[6]

The story of salvation that begins with the groan from a barren womb moves onto laughter and Isaac. The twenty-five years of waiting pays off at long last. Sarah, this ancient of days, gives birth to a comic story. When Isaac is born, Sarah is still laughing, she shakes with the laughter of joy as she cradles in her arms what was once a promise. The word of promise has taken flesh and dwells in their midst. At the birth of her son, Sarah says: "God has given me cause to laugh; all who hear of it will laugh with me" (Gen 21:6). A concelebration of laughter marks the end of twenty-five years of waiting.

Waiting As Process

The story of Abraham and Sarah, our ancestors in the faith, is a story of tenacious endurance. It is not a straightforward, painless story of waiting; the story is nuanced by the couple's despondency, their diminishing energy, their worry about time running out, the sheer fatigue of waiting, and their determination to make alternative plans when the only thing they are asked to do is wait. Yet they hold on, however shakily, to the dream that God has for them; they never give up completely. The day comes when they become what they wait for, loving parents of the gift of new life.

Abraham and Sarah are not only our ancestors in the faith but our teachers. They teach us that waiting in hope, believing in God's dream of us, is not squandering time but hallowing time. In that time of waiting we are being formed. Waiting is our formation. What God does in us while we wait is as important as what we wait for. Waiting is not just passing the time until we get what we want; waiting is the *process of becoming what God wants us to be*. And becoming takes time; there is no becoming without it.

Like Abraham and Sarah, we have to learn to trust in God's providence that good will emerge from all this in God's time. His clock is different, because when he looks at it the units of time are interchangeable: "With the Lord one day is like a thousand years, and a thousand years are like one day. The Lord is not slow about his promise, as some think of slowness but is patient with you, not wanting any to perish, but all to come to repentance" (2 Peter 3:8–9).

God has a different perspective. When an economist read that scriptural passage about God's time, he said to God:

"Lord, is it true that a thousand years for us is just like one minute for you?"

The Lord said, "Yes."

The economist said, "Well, then, a million pounds to us must be like one penny to you."

The Lord said, "Well, yes."

The economist said, "Well, Lord, will you give me one of your pennies?"

The Lord said, "Yes, of course. Just wait a minute."

Often we want God's gifts, but not his timing; we want the penny but not the minute, we want Isaac but not the twentyfive years of waiting. Paul speaks about groaning inwardly, like the whole of creation, while we wait in hope. And he writes: "A hope that is seen is not a hope. For who hopes for what he sees? But if we hope for what we do not see, we wait for it in patience" (Rom 8:24–25). In the meantime we groan together.

Chapter Three

Waiting for Gospel

"Promises, Promises!"

I was traveling on the London underground from Charing Cross north to Euston station. It was late morning and quieter than I had expected and there was plenty of room for my bulky suitcase. At Leicester Square a young couple, carrying an expansive assortment of shopping bags, got on. They were arguing.

She sits next to me in a heap of bags. Continuing a previous conversation, she says to him: "That's all very well for you to say, but you did promise." She seems totally unaware of anyone else, present only to the man who is with her.

Pointing to the mountain of shopping, she says: "Yeah, look at all this stuff, we don't need half of it. And all I want is one thing from you. When do I get the ring?"

He looks up and sees that they've captured the interest of everyone else in the car. Papers and books have been abandoned in favor of this real drama. He says, quietly: "Look, I promise, OK. January or February, I'll surprise you. Promise. Just trust me, you'll see."

She says, loudly: "Promises, promises!"

They sit in silence. The rest of us reluctantly go back to minding our own business. Some passengers take a peek at the assembly of shopping bags. I look too. I don't know what's in them; but I know what small article is not. Euston comes and they are still quiet. I get out, wondering if she'll be surprised by his promise in the coming year. And I think of a stray line from one of Auden's poems:

"Words are for those with promises to keep."

He made her a promise, so he put himself in debt, inviting his girlfriend to trust in him until the day he delivers on his word. Sometimes we promise too much too quickly and we soon learn that we can't deliver the goods. As Ovid observed two thousand years ago, when it comes to promises we can all be millionaires. On the other hand, we're sometimes so doubtful of our own capacity to keep promises that we don't make any. So, we live in the absence of promise, which means that other people have to do the same.

To believe a promise is an act of trust in the person who makes it; it's to live in expectation, holding fast to someone's word. And when promises are fulfilled there is a deepening of the original trust. If people have a distinctly wobbly track record on keeping their word, however, we tend to be cautious about their sparkling new promises.

Of course, we know that we cannot retire completely from giving and receiving promises. Life itself comes to us as a promise, and trust has to be exercised in the midst of the real frailty within and around us. So, when it comes to God's promises we feel hopeful that at least God will deliver.

The longer we live, however, the more difficult it might be to make promises to ourselves, for promises refer us to the future. When we get older, it is easier to consult our memory rather than our hope. Memory is the way we all bring time to mind, and, of course, the thing about the past is that the longer we live there's more of it! As the French playwright Anouilh observed: "When you're forty, half of you belongs to the past, and when you're seventy, nearly all of you."

When we grow old there is a tendency to be long on memory and short on expectation. So we can look to the security of a familiar past with well-known faces and places; we can dig out the photograph albums and page through lost times and be content to remember how it was in the good old days.

When Luke opens his Gospel, he introduces us to four old people who are unusual: they are not looking back at the good old days, but looking forward to the great days to come; their life is dominated by something yet to happen. So they wait.

Zechariah Is Interrupted

Luke sets the stage for his Gospel story by situating the events he is recounting in time and place, both in relation to the Roman Empire, yet he quickly shifts the center of things to the boundaries of that world. As Rowan Williams observes:

> In the first three chapters of the Gospel, Luke deliberately sets the scene by giving us a point of reference in secular history: "In the days of King Herod of Judea" (1:5); "Now at this time Caesar Augustus issued a decree" (2:1); "In the fifteenth year of Tiberius Caesar's reign" (3:1). These are the ways the world draws its maps, with the crowned head at the center of things, the world organized around his presence and measured by his history. In each of these chapters, however, the story immediately turns to a figure or figures conspicuously on the edge of things—a childless aging couple, an unmarried village woman, an eccentric in the desert.[1]

Luke opens his story not in the palace of the Caesars but in the Temple, with the waiting figure of an old priest. In the last chapter we looked at the two figures that dominate the beginning of the story of salvation, Abraham and Sarah, a couple whose life was charged by the power of promise. They waited on a word of promise to take flesh in the midst of their lives. That attitude of waiting eventually becomes the dominant one for the faithful in Israel. The prophet Zephaniah, working in the seventh century BC, speaks of a remnant of Israel who will wait and take refuge in the Lord. Most people will give up waiting on God and attend to their own business, but a minority will not:

> In your midst I will leave
> a humble and lowly people,
> and those who are left behind
> will seek refuge in the name of the Lord
> (Zeph 3:12–13).

Luke will open his Gospel with representative figures of this humble and lowly people, those who are left behind, who put their trust in God and wait on God's promise.

As the story of old, Israel began with waiting figures, so the story of the new Israel begins with waiting figures. Matthew opens his Gospel with the figure of Abraham, the father of Isaac. Luke opens his Gospel with the story of Abraham and Sarah, retelling it through the aged couple, Zechariah and his barren wife Elizabeth. Luke builds a bridge back, to connect his new story of Israel to the old story of Israel, using four waiting figures—Zechariah, Elizabeth, Simeon, and Anna. The bridge between the two ages, the two testaments, is crossed.

Old Israel	New Israel
Waiting on the promise ⟷	*The promise fulfilled*
Zechariah and Elizabeth *Child: John the Baptist* ⟷	Mary and Joseph *Child: Jesus*
Elizabeth greets Mary ⟷	Mary travels to Elizabeth
Simeon and Anna ⟷	The parents and child

Matthew opens his Gospel with a list of names, beginning with the old patriarch Abraham, and travels at a leisurely pace through the photograph album of Jesus' relatives. Luke is much more dramatic, choosing to open his Gospel with a spectacular disturbance in the Temple. A priest, in the middle of serving at the altar, is interrupted by an angel.

To be a priest you had to be born into the priesthood, and there were so many thousands of priests ready to officiate at the Temple that they were divided into twenty-four courses, each group serving for two weeks every year. Not a hectic life, really, when you think about it. There were two sacrifices a day, morning and afternoon, and the presiding priest was chosen by lot. The old priest, Zechariah, has at long last won his only chance to preside at the Temple liturgy by offering a sheep as sacrifice on the outside altar, in full view of everyone, and then going inside, out of view, to burn incense on the sanctuary altar.

Zechariah has waited all his priestly life for this moment: "Now it was the turn of Zechariah's section to serve, and he was exercising his priestly office before God when it fell to him by lot, as the ritual custom was, to enter the Lord's sanctuary and burn incense there" (Lk 1:8–10). Luke's Gospel opens with a lottery winner: Zechariah has won his once-in-a-lifetime chance: probably all the relatives are there to cheer him on and witness this unique photo opportunity for the family album. No kids, of course, but nevertheless this is a big moment for the family.

And after all this waiting for his big chance, what happens? Poor old Zechariah is cut short in the middle of it.

Like so many good stories and films, Luke's Gospel begins with life disrupted: something unforeseen suddenly takes over. The American film director, John Ford, who specialized in making westerns, was asked how a director opens a film that grabs people's attention. He said: "Have a stranger gallop into town. When the locals see this stranger hurtling into their town, their peace is naturally disturbed. They wonder: Who is this guy?

Where is he from? Why is he coming here? And why is he in such a mad rush?"

John Ford could have directed the beginning of Luke's Gospel. A stranger flies into town. Zechariah has not just been waiting all his priestly life for this chance to preside at the altar, but he has also been waiting all his married life for a child. The angel announces: "Zechariah, do not be afraid, your prayer has been heard" (Lk 1:13). The waiting is almost over: Elizabeth is to have a child, the one who has been afflicted by barrenness all her life will give birth to a son. Gabriel then discloses to the new father-to-be a litany of the future accomplishments of his child, celebrating who this child will turn out to be. He will be a joy and delight; he will be great before the Lord; he will be filled with the Holy Spirit; he will be this; he will be that.

Zechariah interrupts the interrupter and asks: "Excuse me, but how can I be sure of all this? Have you seen the wife? And look at me, for God's sake!" Zechariah does what Abraham did before him: he focuses on basic biological laws and the couple's impressive arithmetic, in case angels are unacquainted with mortal problems. The old priest, like the old patriarch before him, becomes fixated with what is, not with what can be, which is why he interrupts the angel.

It is not a good idea to interrupt angels in their flow; they don't like it. Gabriel has no patience for Zechariah's cautionary tale: he believes that old priests should believe the word of God, especially after all the waiting, when it stares them in the face. Thus he rebukes Zechariah by silencing him until the promise takes place.

The Zechariah response is familiar to anyone living in community: the voice that greets new proposals by informing anyone with ears what's wrong with them. Nearly every community has a Zechariah, a demolition expert in dreams, a skeptic even in the presence of angels, a champion of obstruction. When confronted with these merchants of gloom, we should probably follow Gabriel's advice: people like that are best kept silent, otherwise they might start an epidemic of cynicism in the neighborhood.

Poor Zechariah! The old dumb priest stumbles out of the sanctuary into the afternoon light. Everybody has been waiting for him to conclude the service, but he can't say anything. He is supposed to pronounce a solemn priestly blessing over the people. Instead he signs to them in a fit of aerobics and then he goes away, a solemn procession of one, leaving behind him an unblessed congregation and an unfinished service.

When his group's time of service in the Temple is completed, Zechariah goes home a quiet man. Probably the most relaxing months of Elizabeth's marriage when she doesn't have to listen to the old priest practicing his homilies on her! Zechariah's name means "the Lord remembers"—so the good news is that God lives up to the old priest's name and now the waiting is nearly over. About a month later Elizabeth conceives, but the old woman hides herself from the public eye. The old couple wait together, their hope renewed, for what they wait for has now already begun to take flesh. Their waiting is pregnant. As Paul Tillich noted:

> Although waiting is not *having*, it is also having. The fact that we wait for something shows that in some way we already possess it. Waiting anticipates that which is not yet real. If we wait in hope and patience, the power of that for which we wait is already effective within us. He who waits in absolute seriousness is already grasped by that for which he waits. He who waits in patience has already the power of that for which he waits.[2]

The old couple are now grasped by God's word, the promise they know now to be fulfilled. Eight days after John the Baptist is born, his delighted father breaks out of his imposed silence and breaks into poetry as he hymns the praise of God in the *Benedictus*. He blesses God that he visits a waiting people,

❖ that God honors an ancient word "proclaimed by the mouth of his holy prophets from ancient times"

❖ that God remembers "the oath he swore to our father Abraham" (Lk 1:70,73)

❖ that to all those who have waited in darkness and in the shadow of death a new dawn is coming (Lk 1:79)

It is as if Zechariah illustrates the lines of the psalm:

I waited, I waited for the Lord,
and he stooped down to me and heard my cry.
He put a new song in my mouth,
a song of praise to our God (Ps 40:1,3).

The last time Zechariah spoke was to express his singular doubt; now this old priest finds a new song of rejoicing to express his shared joy. He becomes the spokesman for all who have waited in hope, for the *anawim*, the little people who put their trust in God. Because of their waiting, Zechariah and Elizabeth share the privilege of being heralds of the Gospel. As Luke gives them that distinctive place in his narrative, he goes on to note that their child grows up and lives out in the wilderness. Like his father and mother, John too will wait for another day; like his father and mother, he will spend most of his life dominated by something waiting to happen.

John will wait in the wilderness. In his poem, Saint John the Baptist, Sidney Keyes catches something of the character of this waiting figure:

I am John,
I am no vested priest, no savior, but a voice
Crying daylong like a cricket in the heat.
I demand your worship. Not for me,
But for the traveler I am calling
From beyond the Jordan and the limestone hills,

Whose runner and rude servant I am only.
He is not man entirely but God's watchman.
I dwell among the blistered rocks
Awaiting the wide dawn, and the wonder
Of his first coming.

Mary Is Interrupted

When the evangelist John celebrates the beginning of the Jesus story in his Prologue, he says "The Word was made flesh" (Jn 1:4). There is no mention of another human being: no mother is introduced, no time is recorded, no place is noted, no witnesses are named—because, for this evangelist, Jesus' beginning is beyond the cosmos in the fullness of God.

When Luke celebrates the beginning of the Jesus story, he wants to celebrate the beginning of a human story, not a cosmic story. All human stories begin the same, inevitably involving humans. Luke knows that Jesus does not come as a bolt from the blue, but he comes, as we all come, through the womb of a mother. To celebrate the birth of Jesus you need a particular woman: you need Mary of Nazareth.

Six months after interrupting Zechariah in the Temple, Gabriel startles a young fiancée at home in Nazareth in Galilee. Angels seem to have a charism for alarming people with their spectacular entrances, which is probably why, wherever they go, they are always urging their flabbergasted clients: "Do not be afraid."

As the story of John the Baptist begins in sacred space, in the Temple, the story of Jesus will transpire in ordinary space, where people are going about their normal business. Mary is not waiting for a child, but waiting to move in with her husband, at which point the marriage will be ratified. When, like Zechariah, she interrupts the angel to point out that she has had no relations with a man, Gabriel does not punish her. Gabriel is much nicer to young girls than he is to old priests, so he offers a sign that Mary's old and barren kinswoman has conceived a son.

Mary gives the classic response of the disciple when challenged by the word of God: "Let what you have said be done in me" (Lk 1:38). That is her annunciation, her consent to hand over her body and spirit to God's purpose. For the story of Jesus to be told, it needs more than God's word to be spoken, it also needs the human word to say yes. In the annunciation, Luke shows us that the God who chooses Mary must wait on Mary's own response. The love that offers itself is the love that must wait. Even God has to wait for women. Even God needs permission from mothers-to-be if his saving plan is to go ahead. That is why there are two annunciations: God's annunciation to Mary and Mary's annunciation to God. God's best plans can only happen when there is human cooperation, when God's word and our word come together. When those two annunciations come together, God's word always becomes flesh.

Whatever Mary was planning for her life with Joseph, it did not include becoming pregnant outside that relationship. An unexpected word interrupts the routine of life and proposes a groundbreaking diversion from what is planned; nothing less than a startling new future is proposed. Will Mary stay with her own domestic plans or risk an uncharted adventure with God? Mary's annunciation to the angel enshrines her response in consenting to the word of God happening in her (Lk 1:38). Mary gives up her own wishes to adopt God's desire; she gives up personal control of her life in favor of God's promise; in her response she pledges her body and spirit to the purposes of God.

A few years ago I went to Belgium, to visit a priest-friend I had worked with in the Philippines, Father Lode Wostyn. He took me to Bruges to see something of the architecture and art of that wonderful city. I remember stopping in front of a beautiful fifteenth-century tapestry that celebrated the annunciation. It had two panels. In the first panel, God has just sent the angel Gabriel to announce his plans. Everything in heaven stops. The angels hang up their harps, the saints stop taking emergency phone calls: everyone in heaven looks down and holds their breath as they wait for Mary's response. In the second panel, when Mary does say yes to God's plan, you see the whole of heaven let out a huge sigh of relief. You see God wiping his brow, and you can almost hear him saying, "Oh, thank God for that!"

At the beginning of his Gospel, Luke celebrates that something radically new is going to happen: the presence of God is going to become vulnerable in human flesh. In the ancient days it was the Ark of the Covenant that marked the presence of God; the nearness of God was symbolized by the empty space between the cherubim on the ark. Emptiness. Now, Luke says, something new is going to happen. The presence of God is going to take human shape in the womb of Mary. Mary of Nazareth is the tabernacle of God.

Mary, like all mothers, gives over her body and mind and soul so that new life may be born. She does that so that a life larger than hers may take its own place in the world. All mothers must wait for the gradual process that is happening within them, they must learn to let go of the child within them. They must not only nurture the presence of the child within them; they must nurture the leaving of the child. The act of childbirth is the painful act of letting go, so that the life within can take its own separate place in the world. Mary's vocation is not only to hold Jesus within her, but also to let him go, let him become the person he must become.

Mary assists the struggle of God to be one like us. There is something dangerously new about Mary. She is the woman at the center of the Christian story. It is a woman, not a man, who brings God's real presence into the world. Through her the presence of the *Christos Kyrios* will be known and celebrated.

The Mothers Who Wait Together

When the angel hears Mary's response he leaves briskly, mission accomplished. Soon after the angel's departure Mary hits the road south, to Zechariah's place, where she will bring an old pregnant woman out of her hiding place. John O'Donohue, in his poem *The Visitation*, imagines the day following Mary's response to the angel:

> In the morning it takes the mind a while
> To find the world again, lost after dream
> Has taken the heart to the underworld
> To play with the shades of lives not chosen.
>
> She awakens a stranger in her own life,
> Her breath loud in the room full of listening.
> Taken without touch, her flesh feels the grief
> Of belonging to what cannot be seen.
>
> Soon she can no longer bear to be alone.
> At dusk she takes the road into the hills.
> An anxious moon doubles her among the stone.
> A door opens, the older one's eyes fill.
>
> Two women locked in the story of birth.
> Each mirrors the secret the other heard.[3]

The visitation is principally a story of two women, two mothers, the young mother of Jesus and the ancient mother of John the Baptist. Their sons are important, but the visitation is not their story. In this narrative the men are secondary; Luke celebrates the mothers, the ones who carry greatness within them. However important the men will become, however heroic their lives, they will start life like we all did—waiting in the womb of our mother. Unlike the other evangelists, Luke celebrates the role of women in the birth of greatness. All greatness has the same beginnings: it starts in utter dependence on women. Luke celebrates the simple truth that all our lives are a gift from others: who we are is what we owe to others.

❖ Before Jesus and John will carry others, they will first be carried and nurtured by a woman.

❖ Before Jesus and John minister to others, women will first minister to them.

❖ Before they teach others, they will first be taught by women.

❖ Before they cherish others, especially the poor and the weak, women will first cherish them.

For Luke, Elizabeth and Mary are not just individual characters: they represent the whole of Scripture. Elizabeth comes out of the Old Testament, an old woman who has waited on the promises of God. It's not just that *her* time has come; the final time has now arrived in the last of the prophets, her son John the Baptist. He will go before Jesus in birth, he will go before Jesus in life, and he will go before Jesus in death.

Mary, on the other hand, represents what is utterly new and fresh and startling: she is the young maiden, surprised by God. She represents the new Israel, the fulfillment of all the ancient promises, for out of her womb will come the savior of Israel and of all humanity. She makes a journey to meet old Israel. The New Testament crosses the divide and journeys into the Old.

The old and the new come together in the recognition of Elizabeth and Mary. As soon as Elizabeth hears Mary's greeting, the old woman experiences a disco going on her womb as John leaps for joy. The new time begins with womb-shaking rejoicing. Elizabeth compliments Mary: "Yes, blessed is she who believed that the promise made her by the Lord would be fulfilled" (Lk 1:45). Mary stays with Elizabeth three months, until John the Baptist is born. The two mothers wait *together* for the fulfillment of this promise.

Their children will be different. The theologian John Shea celebrates in comic style the difference between Jesus and John in his poem, *The Man Who Was a Lamp*:

> Opposite of the sought-after figure in every way.
> The child is round,
> this one has edges;
> the child nurses on virgin's milk
> this one crunches locusts;
> the child is wrapped in swaddling clothes,
> this one is rubbed raw by camel hair.
> Yet they know one another.
> even exchange smiles.
> They share a mystery,
> this hairy man and smooth child.[4]

Simeon and Anna: Waiting for Gospel

Eight days after the birth of Jesus, the parents of Jesus take him to the Temple in Jerusalem, where they meet two waiting people, Simeon and Anna. As old people they are connected with the past of promise and with memory; Luke presents them as *anawim*—the devout remnant of those who wait on the ancient promises of God. The words of the prophet Isaiah catch the promise Simeon and Anna were waiting for:

> I will make you the light of the nations
> so that my salvation will reach to the ends of the
> earth (Is 49:6).

> Break into shouts of joy together,
> You ruins of Jerusalem;
> For the Lord is consoling his people,
> Redeeming Jerusalem.

The Lord has revealed his holy arm
in the sight of the Gentiles,
and all the ends of the earth
will see the salvation that comes from God
(Is 52:9–10).

Simeon and Anna have spent their lives in longing to see the fulfillment of those promises. They are an unusual couple of old people because their total concern is for the future. They don't live backwards, but forwards. Something yet to happen draws their lives onwards. They are alive with expectation and hope, waiting for the one who will be the consolation of their own people and the light for the Gentiles. They are an old couple that are totally open: they hunger for the future of promise, and wait for the day when they can see it themselves.

Their waiting is not in vain. As Luke says, the parents come with the child Jesus to the Temple. Luke presents them as a good Jewish family that observes the Law, a law that obliged them to consecrate to God the first male that opened the womb. After the tribe of Levi was consecrated to God, however, the parents of firstborn male children were released from that demand: instead they were required only to pay a small "ransom" to the priest to buy back the child. This is what prompts the journey to the Temple.

So, we have the meeting between youth and old age; between the young mother and the old venerables; between fulfillment and waiting. You watch Simeon take the child into his arms; you watch old age reach out for the flesh of a promise fulfilled, gathering this promise into his quieting arms. And you hear him, like another old man, break into poetry, the music of the Nunc Dimittis:

Lord, now let your servant depart in peace,
according to your word;
for my eyes have seen your salvation
which you have prepared before the face of all
    peoples:
a light of revelation to the Gentiles,
and of glory to your people Israel (Lk 2:29–32).

The old man need wait no longer because his eyes have seen
and his arms have held the long-awaited promise of God. Luke
uses this old prophet as a spokesman for his radical theology. In
Matthew's Gospel, Jesus comes from Abraham; Jesus remains
within the Jewish story and will minister only to "the lost sheep
of the house of Israel" (Mt 15:24). Luke breaks out of the confines of the Jewish story: Jesus is not only the glory of Israel,
but also a light for all the nations; and Luke will celebrate this
truth by taking his genealogy of Jesus well past Abraham to
Adam, son of God (Lk 3:38).

And Anna: she is like some of the old women who hang
around our churches, praying and waiting, praying and waiting, and watching. Anna is always around the Temple night
and day. She makes herself God's neighborhood watch, and she
has an energetic nose for what was happening in her neighbor's
house. An inquisitive woman of faith, she is on permanent lookout. Her timing is exquisite, since, Luke says, "She came by just
at that moment"—she has been hanging around for years! This
wonderful attentive old woman now carries the story to all who
have been waiting for the redemption of Jerusalem. The waiting is over; the Gospel begins.

Advent: Setting the Tone

Zechariah and Elizabeth, Simeon and Anna, these old people
are our teachers: they are the ones who hold out, who hang
around, who wait in stubborn hope for Gospel.

The opening of the liturgical season of Advent is the time when we are reminded as Christians that we have to wait for God together as a community of hope. Advent sets the tone not only for the solemnity of Christmas, when we welcome the beginning of the Gospel, but also for the whole liturgical year. Advent reminds us of our radical poverty before God. Advent orientates each liturgical year theologically, reminding us that we cannot grasp God, we cannot possess God, we cannot see God. Like the old people at the beginning of Luke's Gospel, we can only wait for God to let himself be known.

Throughout the year the Christian world congregates each week in a wide variety of communities, its act of gathering together a visible protest against individualism and a counter to the belief that people can best manage by relying on their own resources. In the ancient Armenian liturgy the priest would begin the celebration of the Eucharist not only by bowing to the altar but bowing to the people, acting out the belief that Christ is already present in the body of Christ assembled. The profound bow acknowledged that *in this place* people's identity is not dependent on what work they do or on what career advances they have secured; rather, they are reverenced for who they are in being children of God.

A similar liturgical gesture is incorporated into the celebration of a solemn Mass when, after the priest incenses the altar and the gifts of bread and wine, the thurifer bows to the people and then incenses them. Where else but in the Christian liturgy are people reverenced and incensed for who they are?

At the heart of every liturgy, there is structured dissent from the pervading culture of narcissism: the belief is expressed, through a community setting of narration and performance, that we all should have a greater power than ourselves to genuflect before, something grander than our own experience to bow down before, something higher than our own insight to acknowledge, something that is beyond us yet is mysteriously part of ourselves.

And when we wait for God, it is not only a confession of our incompleteness but an acknowledgment that there is always more to God than what we can know or believe or sense. In that recognition there is a proclamation of hope in the majestic goodness of God: in waiting we declare our hope in God's kind purposes.

Advent disposes us to wait for God in prayerful hope. Edwina Gateley's psalm—*Let Your God Love You*[5]—catches this prayerful attitude well:

> Be silent.
> Be still.
> Alone.
> Empty.
> Before your God.
> Say nothing.
> Ask nothing.
> Be silent.
> Be still.
>
> Let your God
> Look upon you.
> That is all.
> God knows
> God understands.
> God loves you
> With an enormous love,
> And only wants
> To look upon you
> With that love.
> Quiet.
> Still.
> Be.
>
> Let your God—
> Love you.

Chapter Four

Waiting in Passion

The Passion As Central Story

One of things we notice when reading the Gospels is that
the narratives are all heading for the same place: they are
all targeted on the principal story about Jesus, his passion and
death. In Mark's Gospel, when people ask Jesus *who he is*, he
tells them *where he must go*. When people ask about his *identity*, he tells them about his *destiny*: that he must suffer and be
rejected by the chief priests and the elders, and be put to death.
The identity of Jesus and his destiny are tied intimately together.

Three passion predictions (Mk 8:31; 9:31; 10:33–34), at
three "stations" on the way to Jerusalem, focus on the way of
suffering that cannot be avoided. The first prediction happens
at Caesarea Philippi; the second occurs as Jesus and the disciples pass through Galilee; the third takes place as they are
going up to the city. The three predictions prepare the reader to
interpret the death of Jesus: what is going to happen in Jerusalem is not some brutal misadventure, but part of the predeter-
mined plan of God.

In Mark's Gospel, the disciples do not come to understand
Jesus in his lifetime; no one understands who Jesus is until after
his death. And only then does a human being, for the first time,
announce who he is. This person is not a disciple, but a pagan
soldier: "Truly this man was Son of God" (Mk 15:9). It seems
curious that Jesus' identity is recognized not when he is the subject of powerful verbs in his ministry, such as healing or teaching

with authority, but when he is the exposed object of cruel attention in his passion. All that the centurion could see was not the active Jesus doing decisive things, but the victim having things done to him. Yet, paradoxically, it is the victim hanging on the cross at Golgotha, not the radiant Jesus transfigured on Mount Tabor, that calls forth the human recognition of who he really is as Son of God.

The identity of Jesus is known only when his destiny is fulfilled on the cross. This explains why, amid all the images of Jesus that have come down to us, the figure on the cross is the most enduring. That image, above all others, captures who he is.

In each Gospel, the longest story about Jesus is his passion and death. Early on in his public ministry, given the negative reaction of the religious authorities to his deeds and words, Jesus saw his own death as likely. As the ministry continued, so the hostility deepened; there comes the time of painful realization when Jesus sees his death not only as likely but as inevitable.

Jesus is seen to head consciously for Jerusalem, the place of reckoning where he must come face to face with the consequences of being himself. It is in Jerusalem that he will keep an ancient appointment with his whole prophetic vocation: "I must go on my way today and tomorrow and the day following; for it cannot be that a prophet should perish away from Jerusalem" (Lk 13:33).

The passion narrative is the one part of the Gospels where there is most agreement among the evangelists. Scholars argue that they are the oldest stories in the Gospels. Oral tradition about Jesus' death was formed very quickly in the Christian communities: the setting that formed them was probably liturgical recitation of the final days of Jesus, when people came together to hold holy the memory of their Lord. The memory of Jesus that we still hallow is a memory associated above all with the last days of his life.

Journeying to Gethsemane

The immediate context for the passion story is Gethsemane, the olive grove where Jesus asks his disciples to wait with him and pray. Following the Last Supper, Mark has a transitional scene that moves the action from the upper room to Gethsemane, situated on the western slopes of the Mount of Olives. Jesus and the disciples leave the city; nothing is said about Judas. The group would have to cross the Kidron, a narrow valley separating the walled city from the Mount of Olives. At the time of Jesus, part of the valley was used as a graveyard, and when you visit the site today you can still see monumental tombs along the way. Although the journey to Gethsemane takes place at night, the time of Passover would have meant a full moon. After the singing, the setting is suddenly somber and strained: Jesus and his disciples walk through a graveyard and have an argument about how the disciples will conduct themselves during the impending crisis.

Jesus says to them, "You will all become deserters"—a warning that literally speaks of their being scandalized at him. The sense of the Greek word *scandalizein* means "to be an obstacle" or "to cause offense." Before the night is out, Jesus will become a scandal to his own community and they will lose faith in him; they will wait with him no longer, but abandon him to the arresting party. That sad truth is interpreted in terms of the prophecy of Zechariah 13:7: God will strike the shepherd and the sheep will be scattered. The prophecy of the disciples' abject failure is balanced by a promise that Jesus will not abandon his wayward community. After he is raised up, he will go before them to Galilee—a promise that is repeated by the young man in the tomb (Mk 16:7). This pledge looks beyond separation and flight to a time of new attachment with the Lord, to a place where the disciples were originally appointed to take up Jesus' proclamation of the kingdom of God.

Peter ignores the good news that the scattered flock will be gathered together again; instead, he objects to the negative prophecy that points to the defection of all the disciples. Peter grants Jesus the point that the other disciples could desert him, but he professes himself to be a notable exception: "I will not." Peter seems unable to imagine himself in the role of a defector. As if to aid his disciple's imagination, Jesus gives him details of when and what form his defection will take place. Peter will not have to wait long: this very night, before the cock crows twice, Peter will deny his master three times. Peter protests vehemently at Jesus' detailed prophecy. He seems to believe in the real possibility that he might have to die with Jesus. In spite of that prospect, he confidently maintains that he will not deny Jesus. The vehemence of his protestation does not make it anymore truthful, as events will show. The other disciples join Peter in a chorus that denies the reality of their moral frailty. Jesus' inner circle is united against him.

The disciples' genuine attachment to Jesus seems to make them unrealistic about their own capabilities. Jesus has attempted to introduce his own community to the reality of their fragility; they have responded with concerted denial. His attempt to face what is ahead is characterized by both candor and compassion: their abandonment of him will not be reciprocated by his abandonment of them. It is *this* particular community with whom he has shared the Last Supper; it is *this* community who will abandon him; it is *this* community he is pledged to lead after the resurrection.

Waiting in Gethsemane

Mark develops the scene in Gethsemane with a dramatist's care as he graphically depicts the widening gap between Jesus and the disciples. This is the last time Jesus and the disciples are together in this Gospel. The scene begins as Jesus and the disciples enter Gethsemane together; it ends with Jesus and the disciples going their separate ways. Mark accounts for the ending by telling two stories: the story of the disciples' chronic failure to pay attention to Jesus' torment and the story of Jesus' gradual alienation from his own community as he struggles to discern and accept his Father's will.

He goes off by himself, falls on the ground, and awaits an answer to his prayer: "Abba, Father, all things are possible for you. Take this cup away. But let it be as you, not I, will it" (Mk 14:36). Geographically, this olive grove is well placed for escape. Although it faces westward across the Kidron Valley to the Temple, Jesus could turn his back on the Temple, climb the Mount of Olives in fifteen minutes, and head into the Judean wilderness which lies immediately east. No arresting party would follow him into the wilderness at night.

Jesus' expressed desire is for escape. He dreams of making a quick exit, to avoid the misery of staying in place and facing the time ahead. He wants out of the waiting game, so he prays, imploring his Father to spare him and beseeching his disciples to help him find an answer to his predicament. But, as Mark notes in his telling phrase, "They could find no answer for him" (Mk 14:40).

In this case the waiting is profoundly distressing. Jesus is waiting for a prayer to be answered; he is waiting for the time of terror to begin. People who have survived torture tell us that the time of waiting is a time of absolute dread: it is a time when you become unnerved, when everything is thrown into doubt— your own identity, your own sense of purpose, your own capacity to survive and hold onto what you believe in.

Sue Monk Kidd reflects on a moment of insight: "Last year I met with a few of the monks of the Abbey of Gethsemani, the monastery where Merton had lived. As the conversation turned to waiting, Brother Anthony leaned forward in his chair. 'Contemplative waiting is consenting to be where we really are,' he explained. 'People recoil from it because they don't want to be present to themselves. Such waiting causes a deep loneliness to surface, a feeling of being disconnected from oneself and God.

At the depths there is fear, fear of the dark chaos within ourselves.'"[1]

Jesus is certainly disconnected. He asked his disciples to
wait with him and pray, to wait together as a community, but
his own disciples exclude themselves from his drama of attentive waiting. Not only do they not wait and watch with Jesus,
they do not wait and watch with one another. They are afraid
of "the dark chaos within themselves." Often part of the burden of suffering is that people don't talk to one another. Even
though they might be together in the same family or community they can remain isolated and mute, sharing their pain with
no one, simply blocking it out.

As Shakespeare advises in *Macbeth*:

Give sorrow words; the grief that does not speak
Whispers the o'erfraught heart and bids it break.[2]

The disciples do not give sorrow words; their grief does not
speak but is covered in sleep. This does not mean that the disciples are sleeping because they are tired—or, as some have suggested, because they were all drinking at the Passover feast! The
disciples' sleep is the sleep that attempts to exclude painful reality. This is what the ancient Greeks called "elected blindness,"
not wanting to know, choosing not to pay attention. The disciples choose not to stay awake and wait with their leader, because that waiting is so agonizing that it is unbearable.

A compelling image of elected blindness comes from a modern passion narrative, Brian Keenan's book, *An Evil Cradling*.
It tells the story of what happens to an innocent man who is
taken hostage and made to pay for the sins of other people. In
1985, Brian Keenan left Ireland and traveled to Beirut, as a
change from his native Belfast, to teach English. He was kid-
napped by fundamentalist Shi'ite Muslims and kept as their
hostage for four and one-half years; his book narrates his raw
agony of waiting during that time.

He writes about an American hostage, a man called Frank Reid. The kidnappers thought he was CIA, kept him apart from the others, and tortured him incessantly. When Frank Reid rejoined the other hostages, Keenan writes:

> Frank sat quiet and preoccupied behind his blindfold. Frank never revealed his eyes to us. He would always sit in the years ahead, on the occasions when we were with him, with his blindfold on. It was for him like a child's security blanket. Behind it he was safe, he could not be seen; behind it he traveled in his own space and time, occasionally returning to us to join in conversation. Frank rarely entered into a conversation spontaneously. Only when a question was put to him directly would he answer. Always his response was short.[3]

That tells the story of a man who had suffered so much that he had no energy to attend to the suffering of others. His elected blindness is completely understandable; one has to respect those who suffer *in extremis*. It is as if this blindfolded hostage illustrates the pain of the psalmist:

> Friend and neighbor you have taken away:
> My one companion is darkness (Ps 87:18).

In this context the sleep of the disciples is not surprising: their one companion is not Jesus, but the preferred darkness of sleep. The mighty prophet they followed for three years is now reduced to being a beggar. The one who took on the religious authorities, who opposed the powers of darkness, who seemed able to take on the world—this man now seems intent on flight. It is gruelling to watch your leader lying on the ground, begging God to escape. Jesus' posture of collapse and his prayer of desperation hardly promote confidence in his disciples. It is difficult to wait with those who suffer, to pay attention to their plight, to be attentive; it is even more difficult when that person is your leader.

In the accounts of Mark and Matthew, Jesus' threefold journey to the sleeping disciples indicates the time of this trial. It is only Luke who refers to this time as the *agonia* of waiting (Lk 22:44). The Letter to the Hebrews 12:1 compares the Christian struggle to running "the race (*agon*) that is before us." The Greek word, *agonia*, is likewise borrowed from the Olympic games— it refers to what the athlete endures before the race begins, as he prepares for the great trial of strength. *Agonia* means the physical and psychological tension the athlete endures as he is waiting to begin a race, the outcome of which is unknown.

Yet Jesus' prayer eventually turns away from thoughts of escape and turns to consent; he chooses to be where he is, in this painful place of waiting. Through his prayer he comes to a decision not to flee from this *agonia*; he will endure the trial ahead. Thus he waits until the arresting party arrives. In his prayer Jesus does what the disciples do not do: he pays attention to his real situation. As Simone Weil observed: "Absolutely unmixed attention is prayer."[4] Jesus gives unmixed attention to his situation; he changes his mind, moving away from his original desire to escape to a decision to remain where he is; meanwhile, the disciples sleep and so remain unchanged.

In his decision to remain Jesus reckons that the suffering will be overcome only if it is accepted; that the feeling of being abandoned by God will be conquered only if he endures it; that the experience of rejection will be transformed only if he embraces it. There is no quick fix; there is no flight from pain; there is now the willingness to be present to this agonizing time.

And when the arresting party arrives, his disciples can no longer wait with their master; instead they reach a quick community decision to abandon him and leave him to his fate. They hurry away into the night, leaving Jesus to face his time of terror alone. They do not endure. The story of Gethsemane is a story of Jesus' waiting in isolation. To endure the burden of suffering often means to endure the pain of being isolated. Greek tragedy illustrates this growing isolation: relationships gradually dissolve, one by one, until the individual is finally abandoned and left alone. That is Jesus' tragedy. As Shakespeare observed:

> Yet he that can endure
> To follow with allegiances a fall'n lord.
> Does conquer him that did his master conquer,
> And earns a place i' the story.[5]

In the Passion narratives of the Synoptic Gospels, the male disciples of Jesus do not earn a place in the passion story: they cannot follow their fallen lord with allegiance, so they disappear from the narrative as a group.

Gethsemane is an image of sorrowful waiting, of being present to the prospect of what people will do to you; but it is also a story of resolve to endure, literally to hang in there. And this is very difficult to do. Half the world lives in Gethsemane, and the other half is asleep. It is difficult to stay awake to the suffering of others and to wait with them; we want to get on with life, as if life is somewhere else, at an address safely distant from suffering.

In the face of other people's pain the temptation is to become apathetic. As my former professor, Dorothee Soelle, noted:

> *Apatheia* is a Greek word that literally means nonsuffering, freedom from suffering, a creature's inability to suffer. According to the lexicon the term relates to certain symptoms of illness and is translated "insensibility, apathy." Apathy is a form of the inability to suffer. It is understood as a social condition in which people are so dominated by the goal of avoiding the suffering that it becomes a goal to avoid human relationships and contacts altogether....The desire to remain

free from suffering, the retreat into apathy, can be a kind of fear of contact. One doesn't want to be touched, infected, defiled, drawn in. One remains aloof to the greatest possible extent, concerns himself with his own affairs, isolates himself to the point of dullwittedness.[6]

The story of Jesus' passion will go in the opposite direction: it will face the trial ahead rather than retreat into apathy; it will endure the pain rather than escape into avoidance. Gethsemane for Jesus is a crucial decision: he is going to wait it out. Before he is handed over by Judas, Jesus makes a decision to hand himself over into the hands of his enemies.

The Language of the Ministry

Jesus is the subject of active verbs: he makes things happen: From the arrest of Jesus, there is a marked change in the language of the Gospels: as the story moves from ministry to passion, so the language shifts from the active voice to the passive voice. During the public ministry, Jesus is presented as the subject of what is done; during the passion he is presented as the object of what is done.

In the public ministry Jesus is the protagonist whose leadership is demonstrated through the unique authority of his deeds and words, a commanding presence who gives definition to his mission by his vigorous actions and teaching. Jesus is always on the move, and what he does or says is seen to transform a situation: wherever he goes, his presence is a transforming power. He initiates change. His identity, like that of every human being, is gradually revealed through his actions and words. So, for example, we learn about Jesus through his active verbs:

❖ he teaches with authority
❖ he gathers chosen disciples to be with him
❖ he preaches the kingdom of God

❖ he heals the sick
❖ he raises the dead
❖ he stills the storm
❖ he proves himself lord of the Sabbath
❖ he exercises power over the demons
❖ he eats with tax collectors and sinners
❖ he feeds multitudes of people
❖ he prays to God as "Abba"
❖ he confronts and criticizes the religious authorities

The Language of the Passion

Jesus is the object of passive verbs: things happen to him: The Passion narrative tells a different story. One of the most frustrating things about being a victim of violence, suffering at the hands of hostile people, is that things happen to you over which you have no control. The pictures we see of innocent victims of war tell the same predictable story throughout the world: you see mothers running away from explosions, tugging screaming children after them, all desperate for temporary shelter; you see families sitting amid a pile of ruins that used to be their home, wondering uselessly what they have done to deserve this brutality; you see patients lying seriously wounded in makeshift hospitals, photographed and filmed by passing journalists who will decorate their newspapers and news stories with these pictures of sorrow.

When you are a victim of violence you are no longer in charge; other people make decisions and do things to you; you are left to suffer the consequences of their actions. It is interesting to watch the language of the Passion story, particularly in Mark's Gospel, describe what happens to Jesus. It shifts to the passive voice as you watch others take charge of Jesus' life.

The shift is noted well in a wonderful book by Canon W. H. Vanstone, *The Stature of Waiting*:

Mark and John identify the handing over of Jesus with his transition from action to passion, or his entry into passion. But the word "passion" must be properly understood. We normally equate the passion of Jesus with his "suffering"; and at an earlier phase in the development of our language that equation was probably not misleading. For in that phase the word "to suffer" meant hardly more than "to have something happen to one," "to be the one to whom something happens" or, perhaps, "to let something happen to one."

But to the ears of the man of today the word "suffer" has an immediate and inevitable connotation of pain or distress or loss. The translators of the New English Bible recognize this; and in both passages they have made no use of the word. They have recognized that the verb "to suffer" is no longer an appropriate translation of the Greek verb πάσχω which appears in the two passages....

To be faithful to the Gospel record we must reserve the expression "the passion of Jesus" for that distinct phase of his life into which he entered when he was handed over to wait upon and receive the decisions and deeds of men, to become an object in their hands. What happens in both Mark and John when Jesus is handed over is not that he passes from success to failure, from gain to loss or from pleasure to pain: it is that he passes from doing to receiving what others do, from working to waiting, from the role of subject to that of object and, in the proper sense of the phrase, from action to passion.[7]

You watch the movement of the narrative as it describes what happens to Jesus:

❖ he is handed over by Judas
❖ he is arrested and led away
❖ he is abandoned by his disciples
❖ he is handed over to the high priest
❖ he is interrogated and accused falsely
❖ he is condemned as deserving death
❖ he is spat on and struck
❖ he is renounced by Peter
❖ he is led away and handed over to Pilate
❖ he is tried
❖ he is rejected in favor of Barabbas
❖ he is flogged
❖ he is mocked as a king
❖ he is handed over to be crucified
❖ he is led away by the soldiers
❖ he is helped by a stranger
❖ he is crucified
❖ he is derided by passersby
❖ he is mocked by the chief priests
❖ he is taunted by the cocrucified

Jesus makes the transition from working to waiting, from action to passion, from making things happen to having things happen to him.

From Action to Passion

You watch this figure hang on this fixed cross between heaven and earth. The motto of the Carthusians is *Stat crux, dum volvitur orbis*—the cross stands while the world turns. On Golgotha everything seems to move except the figure of Jesus. You watch as Jesus makes a painful transition:

❖ from being the one who healed to being the wounded one

❖ from being the charismatic leader who commanded his disciples, "Follow me," to being the condemned criminal who is now alone

❖ from being the one who invited people, "Let anyone who thirsts come to me and drink," to the one who now cries out, "I thirst."

❖ from being the one who called out, "Come to me all you who labor and are overburdened and I will give you rest," to being the one who now cries out, "My God, why have you abandoned me?"

That powerful transition is one that is not confined to the mount of Golgotha, but is one which everyone experiences in life. You could see that image of transition from action to passion dramatically happen on Tuesday, September 11, 2001. At Hawkstone it was our first full day of the new course, when our large group of international participants were settling into their new surroundings; but other events in the United States dominated our new beginning. On that Tuesday, the day froze—other concerns were left behind. We entered a dreamlike state: we thought we saw this before, on disaster films with giant budgets and special effects—the explosions, the red and black clouds, the crowds running through the streets. But this was real; we were looking at reality.

We saw an image of passion—of people being acted upon, of innocents becoming the objects of other people's cruel intentions. We saw the planes tilt into the World Trade Center where thousands of people worked; the awful impact, the red explosions; the dust engulfing the streets into darkness. But it was what we could not see that was truly frightening. We were left to imagine the human terror inside the planes, in the corridors and the lobbies, and the elevators of the stricken buildings. The terrible waiting. We were left to imagine the horror in the streets below as the buildings later collapsed on firemen and police officers and helpers.

Everything we saw was at a safe distance. It reminded me of Greek tragedy. In their tragedies the Greeks kept their worst moments of terror offstage, out of view, out of the scene. This is the meaning of the word obscene: obscene literally means what happens out of view, because it is too offensive to the senses. We did not see the real obscenity: what was really offensive to our senses happened away from our sight. We were watching death on a vast scale, but we saw no one die. We watched people waving helplessly from windows high up, waiting for rescue, but we did not hear their screams. We watched clouds of acrid smoke cover the landscape, but we were not choked by the engulfing fumes. The horror was at a distance. Watching all this tragedy made some of us feel like tourists at the crucifixion.

In the course of a few minutes thousands of people became objects of terrorists' plans: they moved from what they were doing to become people who were done to; they were catapulted from action to passion. On September 11, Archbishop of Canterbury Rowan Williams was in a staff building of Trinity Church, Wall Street, a couple of blocks from the World Trade Center. He was interrupted. Reflecting on the experience he writes:

> I can't remember much sense of panic, much feeling about the agony going on a couple of hundred yards away, let alone much desire for justice or vengeance. It was an empty space. I don't want to forget that, as feeling returns in various ways....
>
> Simone Weil said that the danger of imagination was that it filled up the void when what we need is to learn how to live in the presence of the void. The more closely we bind God to our own purposes, use God to help ourselves avoid our own destructiveness, the more we fill up the void.[8]

It is that void that is caught so well in the Passion narratives of the Synoptic Gospels; it is a void that is let be, one that the evangelists do not fill in with explanatory commentary or cover over by theological resolution. Jesus enters the void unto death.

Power Not Exercised

Jesus is exposed and vulnerable to everything people want to do to him; he is no longer in control. Yet when we think of leadership we often think of it in terms of control and authority and power. In the language of the Gospel, you expect Jesus as the shepherd to go in front and show the way, to lead, while others follow. In the Passion, however, there is a dramatic shift: the time comes when the shepherd is struck down and the sheep are scattered (see Mk 14:27). In the Passion, Jesus endures what others do to him while demonstrating a unique leadership of vulnerability. As the poet Seamus Heaney observed in this excerpt from his poem, *Weighing In*:

> And this is all the good tidings amount to:
> This principle of bearing, bearing up
> And bearing out, just having to
>
> Balance the intolerable in others
> Against our own, having to abide
> Whatever we settled for and settled into
>
> Against our better judgment. Passive
> Suffering makes the world go round...
>
> Prophesy who struck thee! When soldiers mocked
> Blindfolded Jesus and he didn't strike back
>
> They were neither shamed nor edified, although
> Something was made manifest—the power
> Of power not exercised, of hope inferred
> By the powerless forever.[9]

That curious power, the power of power not exercised, is one that Jesus demonstrates throughout the Passion. The most common phrase in the Passion narrative is that "he was led away and handed over...." That experience of leadership, of being led to painful places, is one that Jesus warns Peter about later, when he gives his principal disciple a teaching about the kind of leadership he will have to face:

> I tell you most solemnly,
> when you were young
> you put on your own belt
> and walked where you liked;
> but when you grow old
> you will stretch out your hands,
> and someone else will put a belt around you
> and lead you where you would rather not go
> (Jn 21:18).

That experience of being led to painful places, where one would rather not go, is one that Jesus first endures himself in the Passion. He now teaches that it is not an experience peculiar to his own story, but one to be shared by those who exercise Christian leadership. In the modern world people like Dietrich Bonhoeffer and Archbishop Oscar Romero have demonstrated that truth, men who were both led to painful places, but whose leadership is honored precisely for that very reason.

> The only violence the Gospel admits is violence to one-self. When Christ lets himself be killed, that is violence— letting oneself be killed. It is very easy to kill, especially when one has weapons, but how hard it is to let oneself be killed for love of the people.[10]

A Figure of Passion

A member of our community at Hawkstone, Father Bev Ahearn, was recently hospitalized with a clot on his lung; he was seventy-two years old at the time. Bev leads a very active life as bursar to our pastoral center, attending not only to the financial affairs of the house but the diverse requests of participants from all over the world. He had just returned from a meeting in Dublin on formation, to prepare for another role as director of the postulants, and was preparing to drive north to Edinburgh for another meeting when he felt an acute pain. He went to see the doctor; the doctor handed him over to a consultant; the consultant handed him over to the care of the hospital.

All Bev's plans were canceled and he became a patient—a word that comes, via Latin, from the same Greek root as "passion." He is passed into the hands of others and becomes dependent on their decisions and actions. From being a very active subject he was suddenly transformed into an object of attention and care. He was examined by doctors, monitored by machines, inspected by medical students, tended by nurses, fed by auxiliary staff, and visited by friends. Things were done for him and to him—he became the still center of everyone else's activity.

Yet Bev, an old philosopher, never felt he was simply an object as he waited as a patient. He shared that he came to a deep belief in the presence of Jesus as the one who speaks, the one who communicates through his word. When the Catholic chaplain came, he declined the offer of the Blessed Sacrament; so secure was he in his belief that Jesus was now present to him as he was, through prayerful communion. On Sunday he attended the Anglican service in the hospital chapel (there was no Catholic service) and found that being present with other patients was somehow more real to him than receiving the sacrament from a passing Catholic chaplain. In the little chapel he was a patient among patients; he was praying together with a waiting community, not communicating alone in his bed.

He noticed, like many patients do, how people visit. Some find it difficult to wait with the patient and, as Bev noted, some kept on insisting on how well he looked, some read his newspapers or finished his crossword puzzle, others commented on the wonderful variety of fruit he had assembled or sought after news about the condition of the other patients. Bev mentioned that in the next bed there was an eighty-two-year-old man, married for fifty-seven years, who was visited every day by his wife. Each day she sat with her husband for hours, two ancient figures, like Zechariah and Elizabeth. Often they would just be together, saying little, smiling at one another, stroking each other gently, secure and comfortable in their togetherness. They waited together, patiently, without fuss, utterly attentive to the other.

Bev made the point that the evangelists make in their own way: that being a patient, a figure of passion, is not degrading; that moving from working to waiting, from action to passion, from giving to receiving, from independence to reliance on others—all this has its own unique dignity. If we measure people only by their activity, what they achieve and what they make happen, we will have no space for the dignity of the Jesus who hands himself over and waits upon the world and upon God. Neither will we have room for the idea of a community which waits on the Lord.

Waiting is an acknowledgment of our own need and a sign of our caring: we wait because what we await matters to us, and while we wait for the Lord we open ourselves to his power and his grace. Waiting, as opposed to passing the time, brings heightened sensitivity and passionate openness. We are more alert, more attentive, like the prophet Habakkuk on his watchtower

> I will stand on my watchtower,
> And take up my post on the battlements,
> Watching to see what he will say to me,
> What answer he will make to me.

And the Lord answered me:
"Write the vision down,
inscribe it on tablets
to be easily read.
For still the vision
awaits its time.

It is eager for its own fulfillment;
it does not deceive.
If it comes slowly, wait,
for come it will,
without fail" (Hab 2:2–3).

Chapter Five

Waiting for an Ending

Living in Hell

Recently someone asked me if I believed in hell. I said that I did. I wasn't talking about the hell of popular religious imagination, like that portrayed in some of the paintings of Hieronymus Bosch. The imagery of Dante's *Inferno*, which he locates at the core of the earth, is much more arresting: the poet's imagery can teach us something about our own lives. Dante's entrance to hell is through a vestibule, capped with the words, "Abandon all hope, ye who enter here." With Virgil and Dante we trudge down through different circles of hell, each worse than the previous one, to meet individuals whose characteristic vices have landed them at their allotted place. After passing through a variety of labyrinthine horrors we reach, at journey's end, the one who is "king of the vast kingdom of all grief." At the core of hell we glimpse a surprisingly pathetic Lucifer, who is encased in ice, weeping from his six eyes, dripping tears down three chins onto the ice.

It looks like Lucifer is encased in his own frozen tears—a depiction not of a powerful, devious rebel but of a wretched, almost pitiable, captive. Like Lucifer, the prisoners of Dante's hell are caught forever in a time without a future; they are *perpetually* waiting, but there can be no release from the eternity of their sentence. Dante's image comes close to what people experience as hell without traveling to the core of the earth— the hell that erupts in chaos and violence in different places around the world, the hell that arrives unannounced in our own lives when we feel trapped by forces beyond our control and utterly powerless to change anything. For many people, hell has a real geography, and the map is themselves.

The French writer Jean-Paul Sartre sought to explore the agony of people who feel trapped in the midst of life, so he wrote a play about hell, entitled *No Exit*. Appropriately, the play is a one-act drama with no intermission. The action opens with three people arriving in hell, which consists of an Empire room with mirrors and no exit. There are no bedrooms, because these people never sleep; they cannot separate themselves from one another because they are condemned to spend eternity together without leaving the room. The three characters are onstage all the time, awaiting the hangman, who never comes. One says: "They're economizing in personnel. Each one of us is the hangman for the other two."

The room is lit by a light that cannot be switched off. At first it looks like a comfortable place, almost cozy. The three characters pass the time reflecting on what has happened in the past, but they cannot grow wise and draw on their reflections to change anything. Still, they continue talking, arguing, and interrupting one another. Hell looks like an eternal community meeting that changes nothing.

As the three people remain locked within the room and the dramatic action leads nowhere, the final line is "Let's go"—the same ending as in *Waiting for Godot*—but none of the characters can go anywhere since they are condemned to perpetual waiting. If people determine their destiny by the choices they make, hell is defined as the place without destiny. For these three, hell is being locked into a past and present that cannot be changed. They have no future, only memories reflecting the past and mirrors reflecting the present. They have no prospect of a time that will be different from the present because they are not free to choose; thus they cannot change anything. They are not waiting for an ending, because there is no ending in this hell.

It is one thing to be locked in a room with no exit; it is another thing to choose to lock yourself in a room because you live in the absence of the one you love, because you live in fear and hurt and disappointment. You never leave your room: outside, the weather reports are always bad; outside, danger awaits you. In John's Gospel this is the evangelist's portrait of the early Christian community after the death of Jesus: they are a community in hiding, gathered behind locked doors, concelebrating a ritual of angst. They have failed to follow their master to journey's end, and now they have become runaways from real life. They have locked themselves in a room that mirrors their fear and uncertainty, a room that provides an unwanted exit for them.

Preparing the Disciples

Before looking at the end of John's Gospel, it might be useful to look first at an earlier scene where Jesus prepares the disciples for his final departure: "I shall not be with you much longer. You will look for me, and, as I told the Jews, where I am going you cannot come" (Jn 13:33).

The evangelist shows Jesus speaking to his disciples for the last time before his arrest and death. Jesus spends his time assuring his followers that although he must go, and although they cannot follow him, they will not be left orphaned. It is the farewell discourse, the last will and testament, of a dying man who is deeply concerned about the fate of those he leaves behind him: "Do not let your hearts be troubled. Trust in God still, and trust in me" (Jn 14:1).

John's Jesus is fully aware of the kind of time he inhabits: "Jesus knew that the hour had come for him to pass from this world to the Father" (Jn 13:1). Throughout most of our lives, we do thousands of things unthinkingly, ordinary routine things that we do every day with no great sense of drama. But we know that there will be a time in all our lives when it will be the last time, the very last time we do things. There will be the last time we open the curtains to let in the morning light, the last time we speak to those we love, the last time we hear our name called, the last time we turn out the light. It is not given to most of us to know when the last time is; perhaps that is a mercy.

In this last discourse John portrays Jesus as someone who is aware not only of the hour but of the effect that this final time will have on his followers: "Listen; the time will come—in fact it is here already—when you will be scattered, each going his own way and leaving me alone" (Jn 16:32).

Jesus' friends are confused and bewildered by all this talk of Jesus' final departure. They will have to face the sudden death of the one they love and follow; they will be left behind, staring into a large absence. Their overwhelming loss will shape the way they see themselves and their direction in life. Their self-understanding as *his* disciples and their direction in following *him* are tied intimately to their living relationship with Jesus. How will Jesus' final departure affect the way they see themselves and the direction they take? An experience of profound loss always makes us question our identity: who are we now that the loved one has gone? Bereavement also stirs up questions about our own direction in life: where do we go when our very sense of direction, which was determined by our relationship with the loved one, seems to have collapsed inward? In the evangelist's imagery, the direction they have *shared* up to the present in following Jesus will be dismantled: they will be scattered, each going his own way. Incapable of following their great teacher on his final journey, they will leave Jesus alone; if they are unable to stay together, they will end up lonely themselves.

In reflecting on sadness and depression following the loss of a loved one, John Bowlby comments:

> Sadness is a normal and healthy response to any misfortune. Most, if not all, more intense episodes of sadness are elicited by the loss, or expected loss...of a loved

person. A sad person knows who he has lost and yearns for his return. Furthermore, he is likely to turn for help and comfort to some trusted companion and somewhere in his mind believe that with time and assistance he will be able to re-establish himself, if only in some small measure. Should a sad person find no one helpful to whom he can turn, his hope will surely diminish; but it does not necessarily disappear. To reestablish himself entirely by his own efforts will be far more difficult; but it may not be impossible.[1]

In the understanding of John's Gospel, it will be the Paraclete, not the disciples themselves, who will "reestablish" the apostolic community: "I shall ask the Father and he will give you another Advocate to be with you forever" (Jn 14:16). The Advocate, the Spirit of truth, will be the gift that will replace Jesus and the power that will refound the community. At the Last Supper, however, this gift is a promise for a future time; before that, the disciples have to face the loss of Jesus and endure the time of their own sadness.

Sometimes the losses we face are so great that they never seem to go away. The Danish writer, Tove Ditlevson, lost both her parents when she was five years old. But what she cherished and held onto was the memory of their presence, not the experience of loss. Many years later she wrote:

> When you have once had a great joy,
> It lasts always,
> Quivers gently on the edge
> Of all the insecure adult days.
>
> The bedroom was an island of light.
> My father and mother were painted
> On the morning wall.
> They handed a shining picture book towards me.
> They smiled to see my immense joy.

I saw they were young and happy for each other;
Saw it for the first,
Saw it for the last time.
The world became eternally divided into
A before and an after.

I was five years old.
Since then everything has changed.

Huge losses can divide time into "before" and "after"; they can become bold punctuation marks that stand out in our story. In the middle of loss it is very difficult to imagine what good can come from it all. Plans that seemed so exciting and important before, now look thin and insubstantial beside the weight of what has happened. Sometimes the loss can reduce us to silence, so we become dumb witnesses preoccupied with our own pain.

Jesus does not want his followers stupefied by loss, unable to move or to grow or to advance life. He wants them to cherish the memory of the time they shared with him, to feed off the good memories rather than be disabled by the sorrowful ones. He knows that they will divide their lives between the before and the after—the "before" when they were with him in Galilee and Judea, and the "after" when they have to live without him wherever they go. He encourages them to believe in him; and if they continue to believe in him they will believe in themselves. He encourages them to believe that they will perform not only the same works as he did, but perform even greater works (Jn 14:12). That is Jesus the great teacher, promoting his friends from disciples to masters, from followers to leaders. Only a truly great teacher can help his students to believe that they can do greater things than he did.

But first the disciples will have to face the time of dark, the loneliness of being left, the feeling of being abandoned when he is taken from them. What will help them in their struggle not to lose faith?

There is a scene from a classic film, from Ingmar Bergman's *The Seventh Seal*, that has always struck me as profoundly helpful in times of loss. A crusading knight survives shipwreck on his return to his native land. He suddenly finds himself doomed; death itself delivers the sentence within a definite time frame. The knight buys a little more time with a chess game, but his soul is sick with dread and longing. Needing faith, he hates his need for it; seeking a sign that God exists, he is surrounded by corruption. He wants to believe, but it is the time of plague, the Black Death.

On the road he meets a peasant couple and their child, and shares a meal with them. It is a meal as simple as a eucharist: they have only wild strawberries—all the food they could gather—and fresh milk from a cow. But love is in the meeting place, in the touch and glance of the young couple, and love's fruit is there in their sleeping child. They even dare to play a song in the midst of plague. And the knight is suddenly gifted with that meaning which is God's gift; the darkness leaves and he says:

> I shall remember this moment. The silence, the twilight, the bowl of strawberries and milk, your faces in the evening light. Mikael sleeping, Jof with his lyre. And I will carry this memory between my hands as if it were a bowl filled to the brim with fresh milk. And it will be an adequate sign—it will be enough for me.

"I shall remember this moment." In the scene of the final discourse Jesus faces the darkness with nothing but his friends and faith in his Father. At the Last Supper, on the night before he dies, before he is handed over to his enemies he hands himself over to his friends. As a Christian community we are pledged to hallow that memory; we remember it each time we celebrate the Eucharist. In solidarity with one another we recall the memory and break bread in his name; we feel a strength that is of God. The Christian community has carried the memory carefully for two thousand years, and celebrated that meal in many forms. We use it for our marrying and our dying, but also for our own journey, week by week, a journey that often takes us through dark places.

Like the knight, we can come to the meal and be gentle for a while. We speak of God and share this food. The bread we take already speaks of God who offers to share his life, like bread that is broken, a cup held out for us. And like the knight we can all say, "This will be enough for me."

Waiting at the End of John's Gospel

The gift of the Spirit to the community of Jesus' followers is variously described in the New Testament as an event that surpasses time; it is depicted as happening at different moments in different narratives. Neither Mark nor Matthew includes an account narrating the gift of the Spirit to Jesus' followers, although Matthew concludes his Gospel with the commission of the risen Jesus to make disciples of all nations, baptizing them "in the name of the Father and of the Son and of the Holy Spirit" (Mt 28:20). By contrast, Luke and John have specific narratives illustrating the gift of the Spirit.

In John's Gospel the apostles are sad at the coming departure of Jesus (Jn 16:12–13)—they are aware that they will have to face the future in his absence—but it is to the advantage of the apostles that Jesus does go, otherwise the Spirit cannot come to them (Jn 16:7–8). The Spirit is called *Para/kletos* (beside/called), the one who is called to stand alongside, the counselor or the advocate. In the absence of Jesus there is also a sense in which this is the Comforter, the one who will console the disciples by replacing Jesus. In the absence of Jesus, the disciples are not left orphaned, but will have the company of the Paraclete.

The gift of the Spirit seems to be first handed over on the cross. The evangelist notes how Jesus is aware that everything is completed as he approaches death (Jn 19:28). As Jesus dies, he hands over the Spirit to the small group at the foot of the cross (Jn 19:30). As R. E. Brown has noted: "In 7:39 John affirmed that those who believed in Jesus were to receive the Spirit once Jesus had been glorified, and so it would not be inappropriate that at this climactic moment in the hour of glorification there would be a symbolic reference to the giving of the Spirit."[2] Following the death of Jesus, when one of the soldiers pierced his side, "there came forth blood and water"—symbolizing the gift of the Spirit. On Easter Sunday evening, when the risen Jesus appears to his followers who have locked themselves behind closed doors, he breathes on them the gift of the Holy Spirit (Jn 21:22–23).

Before the appearance of the risen Jesus, the disciples cannot transform their terror into missionary purpose; they have no power to liberate themselves from the locked room. Like Beckett's tramps and Sartre's captives they cannot say, "Let's go," for they cannot go anywhere. The evangelist John tells us, however, that there is good news in this story: there is an exit from this paralyzing fear because someone else comes to liberate them into new life. Into this room of trapped people, the risen Jesus comes—not to accuse the disciples or condemn them or belittle them, but to offer them first the gift of reconciliation, "Peace be with you." As Jesus proclaimed at the Last Supper: "Peace I bequeath to you, my own peace I give you, a peace that the world cannot give, this is my gift to you. Do not let your heart be troubled or afraid" (Jn 14:27). Whatever hell people live in, the gift of reconciliation, the offering that restores lost peace, is the beginning of deliverance.

Then Jesus shows them his hands and his side: he displays his wounds, identifying himself by the marks he bears of the violence and suffering he has endured. It is a deeply moving picture: a wounded Christ comes to his wounded community. In the last hours of his life, Jesus has been abandoned, betrayed, handed over, led away, interrogated, accused, tried, condemned, led away to the killing fields where he has been done to death, and buried. He did not liberate himself from death: God raised him and gave him an exit from the powerlessness of the tomb.

Now the risen Jesus does the same favor for his followers. As God liberated him, so he, the wounded Christ, liberates his wounded community. The followers of Jesus are challenged to minister to others, to leave their hell of isolation. "As the Father sent me, so I am sending you." The question is this: can we go beyond our hurt, can we minister to people even though we still carry the signs of our own wounds? How can we do this?

The risen Christ breathes on them the breath of God; he exhales the energy of God. What he breathes out, his followers breathe in. The spirit of Jesus is their exit from hell; the breath of God will open the door to a life with others. But the breath of God will not take away their wounds; it will enable them to go beyond their wounds, like Christ did himself, to reach out to those who live captive lives and offer them a real future, one that is different from their past.

Waiting at the End of Luke's Gospel

If John merges Easter with Pentecost, Luke, by contrast, bides his narrative time before telling the story of the gift of the Spirit in his second volume, the Acts of the Apostles. Luke concludes his Gospel by painting a picture of the apostolic community as one that must wait on the gift of God. While the community is commissioned by the risen Jesus to preach the Gospel of forgiveness "to all nations, beginning from Jerusalem" (Lk 24:47), they are not sent out to begin that mission immediately. Instead, they have to maintain a stature of prayerful waiting until their mission can begin in the power of the Spirit, which Luke celebrates at the feast of Pentecost.

For Luke, the time between the resurrection and Pentecost is a time of prayerful expectation for the gift of God who will transform the waiting community into a ministering community.

Since Luke is the only evangelist to write explicitly about the early Church and how it began, he is more concerned than the other evangelists to enable his readers to answer the question: what makes for *Christian* community? How does the Christian community begin? How is it refounded after the passion and death of Jesus? Luke will move his story from a community shattered by the violent death of Jesus to a community preaching in the name of the risen Lord. As a storyteller he will illustrate the movement from the disciples' experience of loss to their new attachment to the Lord. A community that stays and waits to a mission-charged community.

Such a momentous change does not happen naturally or easily. How do you account for the transformation? When people change we often ask them, "What happened to you?" The way the question is posed indicates the belief that something *must have happened* to account for such a change. The question supposes that the individuals did not accomplish this new change by themselves: some outside agency, some event must have taken place for such a change to happen. It is this kind of dramatic change that Luke's narrative describes.

The disciples change because, first, something happened to Jesus: he was raised from the dead by God. In his first letter to the Corinthians, written about the year A.D. 57, Paul proclaims that Jesus "was raised to life on the third day, in accordance with the scriptures" (1 Cor 15:4), yet he adduces no proof to support this claim. This silence is echoed in the Gospel Resurrection accounts, where no biblical proof for the Resurrection is ever mentioned by any of the evangelists, in spite of the fact that there are late Jewish texts that could have been employed and which speak of bodily resurrection, such as Daniel 12. The evangelists' silence is all the more noticeable when compared to the scriptural quotations and allusions that punctuate the Gospel narratives outside the resurrection accounts: there are regular appeals to the larger frame of prophecy which help to interpret an event that might be puzzling, for example, "All this took place so that what was spoken by the prophets might be fulfilled...."

Perhaps the concerted silence by the four evangelists on biblical precedent is thoughtful and deliberate, underlining the uniqueness of what God did for Jesus in raising him from the dead. As N. T. Wright comments:

> The fact that dead people do not ordinarily rise is itself part of early Christian belief, not an objection to it. The early Christians insisted that what had happened to Jesus was precisely something new; was, indeed, the start of a whole new mode of existence, a new creation. The fact that Jesus' resurrection was, and remains, without analogy is not an objection to the early Christian claim. It is part of the claim itself.[3]

In 1 Corinthians 15, Paul goes on to list a series of appearances: no initial doubt is recorded; no words are reported, no appearance is described; no dates or details of place offered; no transformation, apart from his own, is noted. By contrast, both Luke and John introduce physical graphic details in their accounts of the appearances— a portrait some scholars argue that is aimed at countering the Docetist positions that spiritualized the Resurrection. Their emphasis on the physical reality of the risen Jesus is counterbalanced, however, by illustrating his otherness and transformation: to begin with, his followers fail to recognize him. In Luke's account this initial failure is underlined in the Emmaus story and in the appearance to the disciples and their companions. Yet in none of the Gospel Resurrection narratives is Jesus described as a heavenly being, as "radiant" or "aglow" or "shining"—descriptions that are used in the Transfiguration accounts; the evangelists portray him as having a physical body that can be touched (Thomas) and that can consume broiled fish (Luke).

In the story of Jesus' appearance to the assembled disciples and their companions, which follows on immediately from the Emmaus account, the first thing Jesus does is to offer reconciliation in the greeting of peace. He returns to the same community that has abandoned him, betrayed him, denied him, and offers them peace. He is willing to begin again. Perhaps most of us would have returned to such a community to inform them that their services were no longer required, and found a new group of followers! The risen Jesus, however, begins with *them*, the same community, in their fragility. As in John's account, so in Luke's: the gift of peace marks the beginning of this new community.

The assembled group, however, cannot believe it is the Jesus they knew: "In a state of alarm and fright, they thought they were seeing a ghost" (Lk 24:37). Again the nonrecognition by those who knew him in life points to the fact that the risen Jesus is different; he is not immediately graspable. Since their eyes fail them, Jesus appeals to their sense of touch. Again, Luke underlines that the appearance of the risen Jesus by itself does not make for Easter faith. Something more is needed.

Jesus tries appealing to their sight: "Touch me and see"— an appeal that is normally made to the blind. They stand there dumfounded. This is an interesting portrait of a disabled community—one that is blind and dumb: they cannot make sense of what they see and they have nothing to say. The risen Jesus then eats fish before their eyes. This little scene verges on the comical, with Jesus trying to prove himself real to his own community. He then appeals to their memory, interpreting the meaning of what he said during the ministry. Again, there is the appeal to the ancient story—going back into prophecy to try to make sense of new events. He is more successful when he does this, for Luke says that the risen Jesus *opens their minds* to understand the Scriptures.

He gives them a mission statement: they are to preach repentance for the forgiveness of sins to all the nations, beginning in Jerusalem. But he does not send them on a mission, however, instead instructing them to stay in the city until something happens to them: they must wait until they are clothed with the power of the Holy Spirit. *That is the essential ingredient that has been missing.* It is not enough to have the memory of Jesus; it is not enough to have a mission statement. What is needed is the gift of the Spirit.

Jesus tells his disciples, "Wait in the city until you are clothed with power from on high" (Lk 24:49). They cannot arrange this rebirth or manage it by themselves; they have to await its happening as gift. The risen Jesus departs, leaving behind him an unfinished community. The Ascension, on Easter Sunday evening, marks the fulfillment of Jesus' mission and the end of the Gospel. It leaves the community, however, as in-between people: they are between their new loss and their future mission, between their past experience as followers of Jesus and their hope of being a community of Spirit, between memory and hope.

Luke concludes his Gospel by providing an ending to the story of Jesus' mission on earth: in the ascension the risen Jesus returns to God in glory. As J. Fitzmyer comments:

This episode not only forms the end of the Lucan Gospel, but it is the climax of the whole latter part of it—from the crucial chapter 9 on. In 9:31 the transfigured Jesus converses with Moses and Elijah about his "departure" (*exodos*), which he is to complete in Jerusalem. Again, in 9:51, the reader learns about the days that were drawing near "when he was to be taken up to heaven." That *exodos* has now been achieved....The goal and destiny toward which the Lucan Jesus has been resolutely moving has now been achieved.[4]

While the Jesus story is majestically concluded, there is no ending to the disciples' story. Luke speaks of the "great joy" of the disciples—which, frankly, seems somewhat unlikely given the circumstances of Jesus' final departure. The picture of joyful disciples praying in the Temple beautifully mirrors the opening scene of the Gospel, set in the Temple, where the praying Zechariah hears news of a son who will be a "joy and delight" (Lk 1:4). That being said, however, the disciples' story at the end of the Gospel is unfinished: they still have to wait for an ending to this in-between time. They have to wait inside the huge absence of their Lord.

Chapter Six

▄▄▄

Waiting in Absence

The Absence of God and Suffering

A theists do not experience the absence of God: the people who experience God's absence, paradoxically, are those who believe in him. The awareness of someone's absence points, at the very least, to the memory of his or her presence once upon a time: alertness to absence feeds off the memory of presence. For the atheist, God could not be absent, since God has never been present. If atheism postulates that there is no primal source to life and no final goal, the denial of God is an assertion that accommodates that hypothesis. For the atheist there are no ultimate answers to the ultimate questions of life. Why is there anything rather than nothing? Where do we come from and whence will we go? Why are we here? What is the fundamental reason of all reality? Is there something that sustains us and can protect us from everlasting anxiety?

Those who believe in God have a basic attitude of trust in life, a confidence that is anchored in the belief that there is a primal source to life and an ultimate meaning to life. This belief carries over into a number of convictions that affect the way we see our own life stories within that ultimate design: in the fundamental purposefulness of our own life, in a sense of our own worth, in an assurance that we are not abandoned forever, in a wilderness of meaninglessness, to our own devices. As Hans Küng notes: "Ultimate reality itself enables me to see that patience in regard to the present, gratitude in regard to the past and hope in regard to the future are ultimately substantiated, despite all doubt, all fear and despair."[1]

Belief in God affects the way we regard time: we tell time in a perspective that is larger than our own grip on it, wider even than the expanse our imagination can possibly envisage. As Christians gathered in the act of Eucharist, we proclaim by acclamation after the consecration that the past, the present, and the future are radically influenced by the story of Jesus: "Christ *has* died, Christ *is* risen, Christ *will* come again." The sacrament of the Eucharist funds our belief in the nearness of Christ as we listen to the Gospel of the Lord and commune with the one who is the bread of life. Apart from anything else, the Eucharist appeals to the assembly—gathered to "do this in memory of me"—to sense the real presence of the Lord, a presence that is proximate and tangible in the act of communion with him.

Sometimes, however, the real presence becomes the real absence. Sometimes God seems to disappear from the scene, leaving only chance rumors of his presence. The experience of God's absence is often felt most acutely in times of war. The question "Why do the innocent suffer?" is one that has haunted the human race from the beginning. We know that not all suffering is inevitable, that much suffering comes when people are brutalized by tyrannical regimes or abused by their fellow human beings: to glorify this suffering is to applaud the executioner, a stance that is indistinguishable from sadism. Unless we are Christian masochists, bent on the indiscriminate acceptance of all affliction, we naturally protest against the futility of avoidable suffering.

While some suffering enriches and ennobles people, much suffering mutilates people, and they can end up lonely, isolated, and often ostracized. God is often the first casualty in times of personal tragedy, when our ordered world collapses in a chaotic heap of ruins. In the midst of our own affliction, we can find it difficult or impossible to believe what we once cherished: that the world is not an arbitrary place, that what happens is neither capricious nor unmanageable, that there is some majestic design, however mysterious, that is heading for its fulfillment in God's master plan. The unanswered cry is like that of Jesus, "Why have you abandoned me?" Simone Weil defined living in the absence of God as a horror that submerges the soul: "During this absence there is nothing to love."[2] The one we would love is not there; so we are inconsolable.

Other questions are asked, "Why me? What did I do to deserve this?" These questions emerge from a feeling that we have become God's chosen victim; they emerge from an unspoken accusation that God is a sadist and a torturer, arbitrarily imposing suffering on individuals. Something of this interpretation lies behind a curious reading of Jesus' passion and death that sees God the Father deliberately sending Jesus to a violent death in crucifixion. The cross was not the idea of the Father; it was the final solution thought up by religious and civil authorities opposed to Jesus' way of being human and his liberating teaching. God the Father is not a sadist who planned the destruction of his beloved Son in a punitive death; in letting go of his Son, the Father had to be vulnerable to what would happen to his Son at the hands of others, an image developed in the Parable of the Wicked Tenants (Mk 12:1–12). All parents have to take that risk. God the Father, no less, did likewise. Love does not demand the cross, but in the life of Jesus love does indeed end up on the cross. That is what actually happened historically. That is what continues to happen to self-forgetful love. Love chooses not to avoid the suffering that emerges from its commitment. The avoidance of suffering is not love's governing passion; it cannot be.

"Why me?" Behind the question lurks the unspoken suspicion that some mysterious power has selected us out from the crowds to impose on us a sentence of affliction, against which there is no appeal. Whatever it is that causes suffering, it is not love. Love is not the architect of suffering.

In the midst of our own suffering, even when we appear to

be coping in the eyes of our family and friends, we can still feel hopelessly disabled inside, living in a void that seems never-ending, with the prospect of change more than a dream away. Our energies are crippled and our hope is in the emergency room. There doesn't seem to be any way forward; we might wonder if anyone has noticed our profound anxiety. As Emily Dickinson noted:

> A great Hope fell
> You heard no noise
> The Ruin was within
> Oh cunning wreck that told no tale
> And let no Witness in.[3]

When we carry our ruins within us we have no reason to go sightseeing for the architectural ones: we can just journey within and the sight is enough to keep us fully engaged. We can all pass the time inspecting the details of our own ruins, and prospecting for a few new ones. And it's a short trip from there to wondering whether God is the architect of our downfall or, more radically, whether he has retired forever from the human scene.

More often that not, extreme suffering can lead believers to question their basic beliefs. In 1947 a young German soldier died in a Swiss sanatorium. His name was Wolfgang Borchert. During the Second World War he had become sickened of the excesses of the Nazis and he became consumed by illness contracted at the front; his ill health was further exacerbated by torture in Nazi prisons. Before he died he wrote feverishly, and among his writings is a plea to God:

> Has God studied his theology? Who's supposed to care for whom? Oh, you are old, God, you're old-fashioned; you can't cope with the long lists of our dead and our agonies. We no longer really know you, you're a fairytale God. Today we need a new one, one for our misery and

fear. Oh, we've searched for you, God, in every ruin, in every shell hole, in every night. We've called for you God, we've roared for you, wept for you, cursed for you. Where were you then, dear God? Where are you tonight?

The theologians have let you grow old. Your trousers are patched, your soles are worn out, and your voice has grown too soft—too soft for the thunder of our times.

Live with us, at night, when it's cold and lonely, and the stomach hungers in the silence—live with us then, God. Have you completely walled yourself up in your fine churches? Can't you hear our cries through the shattered windows, God? Where are you?[4]

The repeated cry of the German soldier—"Where are you, God?"—is not too different from the cries of the psalmist who screamed on his bed of pain for God and heard only the echo of his scream return to him from the darkness: "Lord, why do you reject me? Why do you hide your face?" (Ps 87:15). When we are confronted with the stark reality of other people's pain and their longing for God's comforting presence we are reduced to silence. Likewise, when we are suffering extreme loss and trying to cope with our own grief, we often retreat into armor-plated silence. There are no easy answers; sometimes there are no answers. Sometimes we have to endure inside a vast silent absence.

Waiting in Absence

At the end of Luke's Gospel, Jesus leaves behind him an unfinished community. This community is powerless to reorganize itself or reinvent itself. They have to do something that is difficult for most of us, to stay with our poverty, to sit with our own powerlessness, to be content with being moved from action to passion. The disciples are charged not to minister to anyone, not to build anything, not to plan. They are to wait in the absence of the one they love, funded by the belief that God's gift of the Spirit will move them to mission. They cannot manufacture their own renewal; they have to wait. Jesus' charge is the opposite of the appeal: "Don't just sit there, do something." Now the appeal is: "Don't do anything, wait."

They have to wait for change. The disciples have already had to face dramatic change, and dramatic change can throw us off balance. We feel all at sea; we lose much of the sense of who we are; we are unsure where we are going. The loss of someone we love can seriously injure our own sense of identity and direction in life: so much of what we considered important about ourselves and about our life now seems irrelevant. The disciples' first loss was the loss of Jesus in a violent death; the second loss will be living in his absence now that he has gone to glory with God. The Ascension marks Jesus' return to the Father—he will no longer be with his disciples in the same way.

Meanwhile they wait; meanwhile they live in the gap, in no-man's land. They are waiting somewhere between grief at the loss of Jesus and hope in their own rebirth.

C. S. Lewis captured the experience of living in loss in his book, *A Grief Observed*:

> Grief feels like fear. Perhaps, more strictly, like suspense. Or like waiting; just hanging about waiting for something to happen. It gives life a permanently provisional feeling. It doesn't seem worth starting anything. I can't settle down; I yawn; I fidget: I smoke too much. Up till now, I always had too little time. Now there is nothing but time. Almost pure time, empty successiveness.[5]

Usually we notice time *retrospectively*, when we pause and reflect how quickly the years have passed, or remark on how people we haven't met for a while have grown and changed.

More often than not we become aware of time *in the present* only when there appears to be nothing happening. Often when we look at our watches we are not looking at real time but calculating how long we have left before we have to be somewhere else. When we become aware of present time, when we check and recheck our watches, it is usually because we feel time is standing still. In the words of C. S. Lewis, there seems to be "pure time, empty successiveness."

The end of Luke's Gospel remembers a time between the return of Jesus to the Father and the coming of the Spirit at Pentecost. It was a strange time for the early Christian community, an in-between time, a time of waiting between the absence of Jesus and the presence of the Spirit.

It is hard when someone we love is taken from us. The word taken expresses accurately the negative emotion of those who are left behind, the feeling of someone precious being stolen from our world, of being psychologically burgled, of being rendered powerless, of suffering decisions that appear to be made by mysterious and powerful others, of being abandoned to survive inside a large emptiness. As Simone Weil writes:

> Even in the case of the absence or death of someone we love, the irreducible part of the sorrow is akin to physical pain, a difficulty in breathing, a constriction of the heart, an unsatisfied need, hunger, or the almost biological disorder caused by the brutal liberation of some energy, hitherto directed by an attachment and now left without a guide.[6]

What do we do with the love that had its fulfillment in the one who is now gone? This experience of affliction is accompanied by the knowledge that there is nothing we can do to change anything. Paradoxically, the present tense is dominated by an absence. When this happens, we can end up spending our time standing and staring at the empty space once occupied by the one we love, aware only of our aching longing for the absent one who has been taken from us.

This is an image Luke uses at the beginning of Acts: "Why are you men of Galilee standing here staring into the sky? Jesus has been *taken from you...*" (Acts 1:11). Jesus has finally gone, and his disciples will never see him again in their lifetime. We can feel sympathy for them when we reflect on our own losses.

My Mother's Death

The scene of Jesus being taken from the disciples triggers a memory I have of the death of my mother. On May 28, 1983, I received a phone call about six in the morning from my sister Ellen. She was crying and said: "Mum won't wake up from sleep—she's gone into a coma and has been taken to the Western Infirmary in Glasgow. You'd better come home." I threw a few things into a suitcase and drove north for five hours, trying to assure myself that my mother was only sixty-nine, with no history of serious illness. She loved life so much, so I persuaded myself she would not give it up too readily.

When I arrived at the hospital the nurse led me to my mother's bed, which had been screened off from the rest of the ward, a bit like a crime scene. Inside the screen the family were huddled together around the silent prostrate figure of my mother. We greeted one another awkwardly and then I bent down and greeted mum, as I had greeted her numberless times before, except that this time, the first time ever, there was no response. She seemed far gone from herself, her eyes unfocused and somehow distant. Nothing moved, nothing seemed to register.

There were no monitors or equipment beside her bed, nothing bleeping or pumping, and it was still too early for cards and flowers and fruits, the clutter of offerings that people bring to the hospital. There was only her in her complete isolation, and we all felt powerless to change anything. There was no illusory comfort of doing something to help—she had already been anointed—so all we could do was watch and wait and pray.

We remained around Mum's bed until evening, sometimes praying, sometimes talking in whispers, sometimes stroking her forehead or hands, leaving for a few minutes, coming back, not knowing, not wanting to know. Each person there was mourning a different loss, because each of our experiences of her was personal and unique. We shared the same hope, however, that she might show some little sign—even the movement of a finger—but there was nothing. There was nothing we could hang on to that might give us ground for hope. It didn't look like she could follow Dylan Thomas' advice to rage against the dying of the light.

I offered to stay the night by her bedside, and the others agreed —they had been there all day—and they reluctantly returned home. The nurses were exceptionally kind and gentle as they washed her and turned her, this docile stranger who was suspended somewhere between life and death. After washing her, they patted her skin with baby powder, something she had done to us when we were babies. Now time had come full circle as she was powdered for her own death.

After tending to my mother, the nurses went back to their stations; they seemed to tiptoe away on their white crepe soles, anxious not to disturb. Then the ward returned to its disinfected silence.

It was strange sitting alone by the bedside, witnessing this lively woman in utter passivity, but in a peculiar way mum's vulnerability now reminded me of what she was and what she seemed to have already left behind her. For a long time I just looked at her, trying to absorb this gifted woman and this gifted time, this mother I had always taken for granted because she had always been there. Now staring me in the face was the stark truth that I had never seriously entertained: that our mother will be taken from us some day and will not be replaced; that there will be an abrupt end to the earliest relationship in our lives; that we will have to learn, no matter what our age, to face life without her being there.

In the middle of loss it is very difficult to imagine what good can come from it all. Plans that seemed so exciting and important just yesterday now look thin and insubstantial beside the weight of what is happening. Not just plans, but the world itself. As Cleopatra says at the death of Antony:

> Shall I abide
> In this dull world, which in thy absence is
> No better than a sty?
> The crown o' the earth doth melt.
> …The odds is gone,
> And there is nothing left remarkable
> Beneath the visiting moon.[7]

As I sat there and stroked her hand, I guessed this would be the last time of being present to her. Early that morning, just before leaving, I had thrown a book in my bag, to help pass what I guessed might be a long time of waiting in the hospital, but now I couldn't read. Reading a book seemed so irrelevant to the present moment. I still have the book and it still remains unread, Thomas Keneally's *Schindler's List*.

Instead of reading I felt compelled to talk, in the mad hope that my mother could hear what I was struggling to say. I spent the night in the half darkness, whispering things to my mother that I wished I had said long before. More than anything I wished that she could hear them now. I anointed her not with oil, but with words I had kept secret for too long, simple words of gratitude and of love.

I have always felt grateful to my family for giving me that privileged time alone with my dying mother. I was unsure at the time if I was waiting for her death or her slow return to life: I was anxious only to use this time, which would never be given me again, for saying a good-bye waiting to be said.

I remember thinking of one of my favorite books, *A Very Easy Death*, by Simone de Beauvoir, where the author recounts the relationship she had with her dying mother. Simone de Beauvoir was the high priestess of the existentialist movement in Paris, lifelong companion of the philosopher Jean-Paul Sartre, and a brilliant writer. Her mother was a simple traditional Catholic, telling her beads and praying that her daughter Simone would return to the faith. Mother and daughter inhabited different worlds, but the two worlds rejoined at the deathbed. The daughter writes:

> I had grown very fond of this dying woman. As we talked in the half-darkness I assuaged an old unhappiness; I was renewing the dialogue that had been broken off during my adolescence and that our differences and our likenesses had never allowed us to take up again. And the early tenderness I had thought dead forever came to life again, since it had become possible to slip into simple words and actions.[8]

I envied de Beauvoir that luxury of speaking simple words to her mother before she died, for the privilege they both shared in drawing their different lives to a peaceful farewell. Did I spend the night talking to my own mother or to myself? Who knows?

In the morning, Ellen returned early because she wanted her own time with Mum, and I left her to her private vigil and went home to catch some sleep. When I returned in the afternoon, everyone was again gathered around the bed, but there was no discernible change. We stayed on, and the doctors gently prepared us by telling us that her breathing was now becoming very difficult. She was going, gradually but surely. She was returning to the shelter of God from which she had come to us as gift.

Just after midnight she was taken away from us. Her death was so quiet, like a leaf falling to the ground; it was difficult to tell the difference between the last moments of life and death itself. The attending nurses moved in, closed her eyes, and drew up the white coversheet to shield her face. It seemed too abrupt to cover so quickly what we would never see again. And we stood there for what seemed an age, staring blankly at this white sheet. No one moved or said anything. The nurses, like ministering angels, waited and then gently moved us away from the covered body.

"Why are you standing here staring into the sky? Jesus has been taken from you...." When people we love are taken from us, sometimes all we can do is to stare into vacancy, into the huge absence that love leaves behind. One person is absent; the world is unpopulated.

Waiting in Loss

The disciples lose Jesus twice. They lose him in death, and they lose him again when he returns to the fullness of God. The disciples may not have become nostalgic, longing for the good old days, but they certainly longed for the new time when he would be with them again, when he would return finally. And they thought it would happen soon. But the Second Coming did not happen as soon as they expected, so they gave more attention to the presence of Jesus through his Spirit. Although there is a real continuity between the historical presence of Jesus and his presence through the Spirit, there is a real difference too, an agonizing one.

This difference is explored poetically by John Lynch in his long narrative poem, *A Woman Wrapped in Silence*. Lynch imagines Mary, the mother of Jesus, reflecting on the difference between the risen Jesus and the Jesus who walked among them, making the point stubbornly that although Jesus has risen, he was not returned to her in the same way as he had been present to her and others before his death. That real loss is acknowledged.

But this was not the old ways come
Again. She knew that. He had not returned.
His presence might be here, or there. They'd see
Him. He was living. He was on the earth
And real, and He had moved again to plans
And to directions. He would speak with them,
And touch them out of sorrow and defeat
Their grief...
They should hear of him. But He had not
Returned. She knew that. He would not resume
As if He had not died, and Nazareth
And Bethany and all the green hills rising.
And the fields were ended. He had done
With them...He was not given back to her,
Nor ever would be...She had seen Him. He had come
Again, and fire was running on the earth,
He was alive, but He was not returned.
She knew that now. She'd seen Him, but He'd not
Returned. He had gone.
He was beyond the hold of any hearth
Or need of place or time. He was her own.
That still was true. But He was not returned...
These were
The hills without him now. These were His roads
Without the hope that he might pass, or turn
A lane to bring a shadow in this sun.
This was the world without Him, after Him,
The silence when his words had all been said,
And He had gone. This was her own place, lonely,
And she'd come to it.[9]

The repeated phrase—"He was not returned"—recognizes the difference between the Jesus who ate and drank with friends and sinners, the one who walked the roads of Galilee, and the risen Jesus who is now in glory. If we talk about the real presence of Jesus, we can also speak about his real absence. Sure, the Spirit continues his presence, but that is not the same. His first friends cried, "Maranatha!"—"Come, Lord Jesus!" That was their cry from the heart, to be together again with the one they loved and lost.

There is a lovely ancient Aztec prayer, which reflects on the preciousness and the fragility of life. As the Aztecs thank the Creator for their life and breath, they acknowledge that their life and the lives of their loved ones are only on loan for a short while. The prayer says:

> Oh, only for so short a while you
> have loaned us to each other,
> because we take form in your act
> of drawing us,
> and we take life in your painting us,
> and we breathe in your singing us.
> But only for so short a while
> have you loaned us to each other.

That prayer celebrates that all of life is on loan to us; it is gift, given for a limited time, out of love. Those we love are only on loan to us. Sometimes we are lucky, and the loan lasts a good while; at other times we are unlucky, and the loan lasts only for three years.

We are called to live in the absence of the historical Jesus: that absence has to be acknowledged. We have the community; we have the memory of Jesus; we have the Spirit. This has to be enough. We have to look to one another, to see in one another the presence of the one we love. We have to cherish the memory of Jesus. And, above all, we have to live out of his Spirit.

Like the first disciples, we affirm our shared hope as we wait together for the fulfillment of a word that has already been spoken, for the completion of something that has already begun. In family and community all of us soon learn that the fullness of life is not available to us with immediate effect. There is always more to life and to people than we can ever manage to absorb at any one time; and we can hold fast to neither the gift of life nor loved ones forever. Thus Luke concludes his Gospel with a deliberate tension—while Jesus' mission is completed, the mission of the community cannot yet begin. What happens to the community that waits in the absence of Jesus? What happens to the community that waits inside its own loss? Luke will leave the answer to those questions until his second volume.

Chapter Seven

Waiting for the Spirit

The Beginning of Acts

In the first book, Theophilus, I wrote about all that Jesus did and taught from the beginning until the day when he was taken up to heaven, after giving instructions through the Holy Spirit to the apostles whom he had chosen. After his suffering he presented himself alive to them by many convincing proofs, appearing to them during forty days and speaking about the kingdom of God. While staying with them, he ordered them not to leave Jerusalem, but to wait there for the promise of the Father. "This," he said, "is what you have heard from me; for John baptized with water, but you will be baptized with the Holy Spirit not many days from now."

The Ascension of Jesus

6So when they had come together, they asked him, "Lord, is this the time when you will restore the kingdom to Israel?" 7He replied, "It is not for you to know the times or periods that the Father has set by his own authority. 8But you will receive power when the Holy Spirit has come upon you; and you will be my witnesses in Jerusalem, in all Judea and Samaria, and to the ends of the earth."

9When he had said this, as they were watching, he was

lifted up, and a cloud took him out of their sight. [10]While he was going and they were gazing up toward heaven, suddenly two men in white robes stood by them. [11]They said, "Men of Galilee, why do you stand looking up toward heaven? This Jesus, who has been taken up from you into heaven, will come in the same way as you saw him go into heaven."

Matthias Chosen to Replace Judas

[12]Then they returned to Jerusalem from the mount called Olivet, which is near Jerusalem, a sabbath day's journey away. [13]When they had entered the city, they went to the room upstairs where they were staying, Peter, and John, and James, and Andrew, Philip and Thomas, Bartholomew and Matthew, James son of Alphaeus, and Simon the Zealot, and Judas son of James. [14]All these were constantly devoting themselves to prayer, together with certain women, including Mary the mother of Jesus, as well as his brothers.

[15]In those days Peter stood up among the believers (together the crowd numbered about one hundred twenty persons) and said, [16]"Friends, the scripture had to be fulfilled, which the Holy Spirit through David foretold concerning Judas, who became a guide for those who arrested Jesus—[17]for he was numbered among us and was allotted his share in this ministry." [18](Now this man acquired a field with the reward of his wickedness; and falling headlong, he burst open in the middle and all his bowels gushed out. [19]This became known to all the residents of Jerusalem, so that the field was called in their language Hakeldama, that is, Field of Blood.) [20]"For it is written in the book of Psalms,

'Let his homestead become desolate,
    and let there be no one to live in it';
and
    'Let another take his position of overseer.'

[21]So one of the men who have accompanied us during all the time that the Lord Jesus went in and out among us, [22] beginning from the baptism of John until the day when he was taken up from us—one of these must become a witness with us to his resurrection." [23]So they proposed two, Joseph called Barsabbas, who was also known as Justus, and Matthias. [24]Then they prayed and said, "Lord, you know everyone's heart. Show us which one of these two you have chosen [25]to take the place in this ministry and apostleship from which Judas turned aside to go to his own place." [26]And they cast lots for them, and the lot fell on Matthias; and he was added to the eleven apostles (Acts 1:1–26, NRSV).

Is the Time of Waiting Over?

At the beginning of Luke's Gospel, we saw how Luke used his first two chapters to build a bridge back to the story of Israel, the Law and the Prophets, demonstrating for the reader a visible continuity between the old story of Israel and the new story of Jesus. Illustrating the prophecy-fulfillment accord between the two stories, Luke shows the ancient waiting figures—Zechariah and Elizabeth, Simeon and Anna—cross the bridge from the world of the Old Testament to meet Jesus and have their expectations fulfilled in him.

Luke repeats his architectural construction at the beginning of Acts, demonstrating the connection between the drama narrated in his Gospel and his new account of the early Church.

He re-collects the whole of the Jesus tradition, for this is the heritage from which the Church is founded, and you watch the principal witnesses of that heritage cross the bridge from the Gospel: Jesus himself, the apostolic group, the women of Jerusalem, Mary and the brothers of Jesus. We will look at the significance of this grouping later in this chapter.

While the Gospel narrative begins in the Jerusalem Temple among Jews and concludes in the Jerusalem Temple among the Jewish followers of Jesus, Luke's second volume, the story of the Acts of the Apostles, begins in Jerusalem and ends in Rome with the Paul's proclamation: "This salvation of God has been sent to the pagans, they will listen to it" (Acts 28:28). The future of the Church now lies more in the geographical spread of the pagan Roman Empire than within the confines of Judaism. Luke's second volume will chart the development of how Jesus' message moves geographically and ethnically: the Gospel moves from Jerusalem to the heart of the Roman Empire, from Jew to Gentile. In Acts, Luke provides us with the basic structure to account for the great transition, how Christians move from being a Palestinian sect to an assembly of diverse communities in the Greco-Roman world.

Luke is not going to begin the story of the Church in the absence of Jesus. The beginning of Acts shows the truth that the Church is rooted in attachment to Jesus and founded in his authoritative word—hence the forty days of teaching. The symbolism of forty connects this time not only to the preparatory period in the wilderness before the Jesus' public ministry but back farther to the preparatory forty years of the chosen people before they entered the promised land. The symbolic image of forty clearly signals this time as a key initial stage, a time of waiting, a time of transition, and a time of change.

As John the Baptist appeared at the beginning of the public ministry of Jesus, so he is now mentioned at the beginning of this new story. In Luke's Gospel, John proclaimed: "I baptize you with water, but someone is coming, someone who is more powerful than I am...he will baptize you with the Holy Spirit and with fire" (Lk 3:16). The unidentified "someone" heralded by John is identified by the early Church as Jesus. Jesus now declares: "This," he said, "is what you have heard from me; for John baptized with water, but you will be baptized with the Holy Spirit not many days from now" (Acts 1:4–5). Jesus reminds his followers not only about what he said but what John the Baptist proclaimed when he made the distinction between his own baptism of water and the coming baptism of the Holy Spirit. The word of the prophet John will soon be fulfilled in a Spirit baptism that will be accompanied by signs of fire.

As demonstrated in the chart that follows, Luke's two scenes of the Ascension, at the end of the Gospel and the beginning of Acts, have different purposes. The Ascension at the close of the Gospel, which happens on Easter Sunday evening, celebrates the completion of Jesus' mission in his return, in glory, to God. The Ascension in Acts, which happens forty days after the Passion, signals the beginning of something new, the mission of the apostolic Church in the coming gift of the Spirit. In both stories Luke, as a storyteller, celebrates in time what happens outside time. As R. E. Brown writes:

> In using the ascension twice Luke shows once more that despite the concreteness of his description he has no naive understanding of what he is describing. The going of Jesus to God after death is timeless from the viewpoint of God; but there is a sequence from the viewpoint of those whose life he touched.[1]

The Two Accounts of the Ascension of Jesus

	Luke 24:49–53	Acts 1:1–4
Time	Easter Sunday evening	40 days after Passion
Place of Ascension	Bethany (on Mount of Olives)	Mount of Olives
Luke's purpose	Luke concludes his Gospel with Jesus' victory over death and his return in glory to the Father. Jesus leaves behind him an unfinished community that is powerless to reorganize itself for mission: they must wait for God.	Luke opens the story of the Church by *showing* that the early community lives in attachment to Jesus and his teaching about the kingdom of God. This is a *community of memory* waiting to become a *community of spirit*.
The final instructions of Jesus	i) **Mission:** Repentance preached to all the nations, beginning in Jerusalem. ii) Stay in the city until Jesus sends what the Father has promised.	i) Not for disciples to know the date of the end of the world. ii) **Mission:** When they receive the Spirit, they must then witness not only in Jerusalem, but throughout Judea, Samaria, to the ends of the earth.
Jesus' departure	After blessing them, Jesus withdraws and is carried up to heaven.	He is lifted up while they look on, and a cloud takes him from their sight.

	Luke 24:49–53	Acts 1:1–4
Disciples' reaction	i) After worshiping him, they return to Jerusalem full of joy. ii) They are continually in the Temple praising God.	I) They continue staring into the sky. Ii) They are questioned about this by two men in white who announce that Jesus will come back in the same way as they saw him go. Iii) They return to Jerusalem, to the upper room. Three groups make up the principal witnesses from the Gospel: he eleven apostles; the women of Galilee; Mary and the brothers of Jesus. This *community of Gospel memory* joins together in prayer.

As a storyteller Luke demonstrates the impact of the risen Jesus, in time, on the early community. Thus Jesus is seen to settle a question that disturbed and divided the early community: "So when they had come together, they asked him, 'Lord, is this the time when you will restore the kingdom to Israel?'" (Acts 1:6). The early Christians considered the outpouring of the Spirit as the principal sign that would mark the end of the world—hence the question. Another question concerning the Gentile mission is included: Is this kingdom restricted to Israel?

Among many of the early Christians there was a strong belief in the imminent end of the world, one based on a saying of
Jesus, which spoke of the community's liberation being near at
hand: "I tell you solemnly, before this generation has passed
away all will have taken place" (Lk 21:32; see Mk 13:30). That
saying emphasized the proximity of the end—that the community would not have to wait long to experience the fullness of
time. This made for conflict in the early Church, for example
between the sedentary apostles waiting in Jerusalem for an imminent end and Paul, the great missionary, devoted to expand-
ing the reaches of the Gospel beyond Jerusalem and Judea. If
you believe the end of the world is indeed nigh, there is little
point in developing missionary programs or writing books.

The statements pointing to the imminent end of the world
were counterbalanced by others that emphasized ignorance of
the exact time. In his Gospel, Luke, unlike Matthew, made no
use of Mark's saying: "As for that day or hour, nobody knows
it, neither the angels in heaven, nor the Son; no one but the
Father" (Mk 13:32; Mt 24:36). Luke preserves that saying until this passage not only to explain the disappointment of those
who shared a belief in the imminent expectation of the last times
but also to give direction to his writing about the Gentile mission: "It is not for you to know the times or periods that the
Father has set by his own authority. But you will receive power
when the Holy Spirit has come upon you; and you will be my
witnesses in Jerusalem, in all Judea and Samaria, and to the
ends of the earth" (Acts 1:8–9).

The injunction of the risen Jesus dismisses the disciples'
concern to know the exact time of the end of the world, moving
them away from an anxiety that will render them immobile to
focus on the challenge of their itinerant vocation. Jesus' command is seen as a Church-founding one, just as Matthew concludes his Gospel with a similar missionary charge (Mt 28:19–
20).

Jesus' statement also summarizes the contents of the book

of Acts, serving as the equivalent of a table of contents, so that the ensuing drama can be seen as a fulfillment of the words of Jesus. Thus the geographical movement of the book is set:

Acts 1–5	Jerusalem
Acts 6–7	Martyrdom of Stephen. The resulting persecution of the Greek-speaking disciples (not the apostles) impels the first missionary outreach.
Acts 8–12	Judea and Samaria
Acts 13–28	Paul's preaching to Jews and Gentiles through Asia Minor, Macedonia, and Achaia (Greece), ending in Rome, where Luke concludes his story, celebrating how the Gospel is preached "with complete freedom and without hindrance from anyone" (Acts 28:31) in the heart of the Roman Empire.

The Gentile mission is not only a human enterprise but, more importantly, a dramatic missionary expansion under the guidance of the risen Lord, answering the disciples' question: salvation is not confined within Israel. Even Luke's decision to write the book can be seen as the outcome of his belief that the end of the world will not happen soon. As E. Haenchen notes:

> In its Lucan form, this saying forbids the asking of questions about the hour of the Parousia. It is evident from this that Luke is a spokesman of a new age. He has decisively renounced all expectations of an imminent end. Consequently the task has arisen of finding a new relationship to this world in which, by God's inscrutable will, the Christians must continue to live.[2]

That new relationship to the world is a missionary one, a dramatic outreach funded by the Holy Spirit. They "will receive power when the Holy Spirit has come upon" them. This expression recalls the angelic annunciation in Luke 1:35, suggesting a parallel between the conception of Jesus and that of the Church. There is a clear continuity between the life of Jesus and the life of the Church, the same Spirit being the creative force of both. Likewise, when the Spirit comes on Jesus in the Jordan (Lk 3:22) it marks the beginning of his public ministry; the coming baptism of the Spirit for the disciples will also mark the beginning of their missionary life.

The Community of Memory: The Three Groups

The ascension of Jesus, however, does not mark the new beginning of the missionary community. When Jesus is taken from their sight, Luke portrays the community standing and staring up into the heavens. This stance is not a particularly missionary one, and the evident danger is that the early Church might end up as a stationary community, focused inwardly, waiting for the end of the world and the return of Jesus. The angels assure the gathering that Jesus will return in the same way as he has gone.

The core group all wait obediently in Jerusalem for the coming of the Spirit. As L. Alexander notes: "'Devoted themselves… to prayer' (v. 14) suggests the virtue of dogged perseverance."[3] They are still defined as a waiting community, one that lives in between the loss of Jesus and the gift of the Spirit. But the significance is that they wait together in a spirit of prayer. At the core of the assembly three groups are mentioned: these are the principal witnesses of the entire movement of Luke's Gospel and they cross the bridge and appear in the opening scenes of his new work, acting as the original link between the life and ministry of Jesus and the new time of the Spirit.

> **named apostles** (covering the public ministry until the passion)
> **women of Galilee** (covering the passion and death of Jesus, and the empty tomb)

Mary and the brothers of Jesus (covering the early life of Jesus)

Mary is the only adult in this group who appears in the Infancy narrative, the only named witness from that period in Luke's Gospel. In his portrait of Mary, Luke presented her as the first disciple of the word of God. If Luke defines the true family of Jesus in terms of discipleship—"My mother and my brothers are those who hear the word of God and keep it" (Lk 8:21)—he shows Mary already fulfilling that requirement before the conception of Jesus. In the Infancy narrative she becomes the mother of Jesus because she is a disciple of the word of God: in response to the angelic Annunciation her motherhood follows on her annunciation, "Let what you have said be done to me" (Lk 1:38).

The brothers of Jesus seem to have shared an attitude of reserve, if not hostility, toward Jesus (see Mk 3:21; Jn 7:4). Paul's statement that the risen Jesus appeared to James (1 Cor 15:7) seems to account for a change of heart. James, the eldest and most prominent of Jesus' brothers, is reckoned as one of the three pillars of the Church (Gal 2:9) and he will emerge as the undisputed leader of the Church in Jerusalem (Acts 15:13; 21:18). Although not identified by name in this grouping in Acts, he is clearly present among the members of Jesus' immediate family.

Luke names the eleven apostles; Judas is missing, but he will soon be replaced. The defection of Judas Iscariot means the community has to find a replacement to bring the number of apostles up to *twelve*, since Jesus chose twelve followers to act as judges of the twelve tribes of Israel. The qualification for being numbered among the Twelve is set by Peter: "So one of the men who have accompanied us during all the time that the Lord Jesus went in and out among us, beginning from the baptism of John until the day when he was taken up from us—one of these must become a witness with us to his resurrection"

(Acts 1:21–22). The new member must have been a companion of Jesus and the other eleven apostles throughout the public ministry, and thus be able to witness from experience to the whole of the Jesus tradition. In this way he can act as a witness "with us" to the resurrection.

Luke seems to make a distinction between the role of the Twelve and the role of the apostle. While the Twelve share with a wider group the calling of being apostles, they are distinctive and exclusive as the Twelve. Although the apostles have successors, the Twelve do not: that office is unique to them and is carried over to resurrection life, since they will fulfill their role as twelve judges of the tribes of Israel. Sitting on a throne to judge others is a sedentary position rather than a missionary one, whereas the function of the apostle— the one who is sent— carries a much more energetic feel to it, of people on the move, those later described as the "followers of the Way" (Acts 9:2). Perhaps this explains why the Twelve, with the exception of Peter and John, remain in Jerusalem. Some years later, when James the son of Zebedee, another member of the Twelve, is executed by Herod Agrippa the elder, his death does not create a vacancy. Although, at the opening of Acts, Matthias is named as the twelfth apostle, you never hear about him again in this volume. For Luke, the importance of Matthias is that he completes the arithmetic of the Twelve.

While the Twelve can cover the period of the public ministry of Jesus, they are not able to cover the period of the passion and death of Jesus. The women of Galilee were the silent witnesses of these events, as they were the first to hear the angelic Annunciation in the empty tomb. They are the visible continuity of the community's witness, which is founded in the authority of their own experience. As the woman Mary was "first at the cradle" so the women of Galilee are "last at the cross." These women are moved from the two limits of the Jesus story, the beginning and the end, and placed at the heart of the core community of the Church. Luke gives them their unique place at the beginning of the Church, because they enjoyed a unique place in the story of Jesus.

These three groups of witnesses—the Twelve, the women of Galilee, Mary and the brothers of Jesus—collectively bring Luke's Gospel in its entirety into the beginning of Acts. Together they form the basic community of memory, the witnesses of Jesus' full story. Together they pray and wait for the day when they will become the community of Spirit, after which they can begin their missionary witness in the power of God's gift.

The Community of Spirit

The community of memory can function as *witnesses* only when they become a community of Spirit. Luke celebrates this event at Pentecost, the Greek name for the Jewish Feast of Weeks, which derived its name from its occurrence fifty days after Passover. Originally in the Jewish tradition the Feast of Weeks concluded the period of seven weeks that began with the presentation of the first sheaf of the wheat harvest during the Passover. Later it assumed historical significance as a commemoration of the covenant given to Moses at Sinai, when God revealed his Law and ratified his choice of Israel as his people. The choice of Israel as God's people was understood to have taken place on the fiftieth day after the Exodus, thus giving the agricultural feast a new theological dimension as the first Pentecost and the establishment of God's people.[4]

Luke uses this great pilgrimage feast to celebrate a new Pentecost in the founding of the Christian community through the gift of the Holy Spirit. Luke has bided his time for this moment, to clarify to his readers that the waiting is ended in the refounding of the community; this is not managed by the members themselves but by the endowment of God. The outpouring of the Spirit at Pentecost enables the community not only to testify to Jesus' life, death, and resurrection, but to the significance of all that this means now.

119

It is Luke who demonstrates the effects of the Spirit in the ministry of the disciples. They go outdoors and proclaim what God has accomplished in the death and resurrection of Jesus. They go to the marketplace where people gather and there they proclaim how they have been changed by the power of the Spirit. They tell a Magnificat and proclaim how God is working wonders in them.

Some of the crowds think the disciples are drunk—no doubt because the crowd knows it would take some kind of spirit to transform these men. Whatever it is, people know that something has happened to the followers of Jesus. They have had a new experience. And the name of that experience is Spirit.

The crowd's other reaction is a joyous one when they realize the followers of Jesus are speaking their own languages, a shift from speaking "in tongues" (glossolalia) to speaking "in different languages"—from ecstatic voices to intelligible speech. The gift of the Spirit is a remedy for the disparity of languages at Babel and the dispersion of the human race (Gen 11:1–9). By contrast, in the coming of the Spirit, the new message proclaimed by the apostles can be received by every nation on earth, thus drawing them into unity.

Perhaps we have all heard people say to us in a mixture of relief and enthusiasm, "Now you're speaking my language." When that happens there is communion, where before there had been only division. The disciples get through to people; they speak the deep language that is in all of us and rarely gets spoken. It is language in search of understanding; it is music in search of a melody; it is a liberating message in search of a hearer. Paul spoke of it as groaning, the cry of the spirit within us. The disciples reach people with this profound language: it is the language of the spirit of Jesus.

In Peter's address to the crowd, Luke is concerned to place these new events firmly in the context of the story of old Israel. As Raymond Brown writes:

Worth noting is the fact that Peter makes this proclamation in what we would call Old Testament terms,
thus affirming the basic consistency of what God has
done in Jesus Christ with what the God of Israel did for
and promised to the people of the covenant. Long centuries after God first called the Hebrew slaves and made
them the people of Israel, their self-understanding would
be tested as to whether anything had really changed
because of that calling, especially when they lost the
land and were carried off into exile. In other words,
they lived through beforehand what has often been the
Christian experience in the centuries after Jesus. Both
they and we have had to have the vision of faith to see
God's realities in and through a history where at times
God seems to be absent. In part that is why the Old
Testament remains an essential element in Christian
proclamation. It covers not only the establishment of
the covenant but the attempt to live as God's covenanted
people over a millennium of ups and downs. The New
Testament alone covers too short a period of time and
is too filled with success to give Christians the lessons
the Old Testament gives.[5]

Moving from proof texts from the Old Testament, Peter
notes that the dramatic change seen in the followers of Jesus
points, first of all, to what has happened to the Jesus they crucified: "God has raised him to life" (Acts 2:23). The return of
Jesus in being raised to the heights at God's right hand was a
precondition for the sending of the Spirit. Thus the gift of the
Spirit is the result and the proof of Jesus' exaltation into heaven:
"What you see and hear is the outpouring of that Spirit" (Acts
2:33).

The Community of Memory and Spirit

Luke's carefully drawn portrait of the Church as a community of memory *and* Spirit is one of the great gifts he leaves us in his writing at the beginning of Acts. The Church is a community forever identified with a dangerous memory of Jesus. That memory of Jesus—who he was, what he did and said, his values and preferences, his death and resurrection—all this gives the community its roots and direction as a *Christian* community. The Christian community continues to define itself as a community of memory when it assembles to hallow the memory of Jesus. In each of the eucharistic prayers, immediately after the consecration, the priest proclaims the purpose of the celebration—for example in the Roman Canon: "Father, we celebrate the memory of Christ your Son. We your people and your ministers recall...."

At the conclusion of every eucharistic prayer, the assembly is invited to declare itself a community of Spirit in the doxology: "Through him, with him, in him, in the unity of the Holy Spirit, all glory and honor is yours, almighty Father, for ever and ever." To which the assembly gives its consent with a robust "Amen."

The memory of Jesus roots Christianity in particular attachment to Jesus. That relationship is a critical corrective to an excess of independent spiritual experiences that can detach the community from its historical roots. Without the memory of Jesus, the community can invent its own values, determine its own direction, and lose its spiritual foundation in the person and values of Jesus. While clearly there is nothing wrong with praising the Lord, there is a stark warning to Matthew's community that "Not everyone who says to me 'Lord, Lord,' will enter the kingdom" (Mt 7:21ff). There is always a danger that the community might become disconnected from its life-giving source and lose its direction in individual ecstatic experiences, rather than building its house securely on the word of Jesus.

To counter this danger, Luke sees the Church as a community that is vibrantly linked through a chain of people and faith back through the apostles to the person of Jesus; it is a community that always gathers in the name of Jesus, not in its own name. The ecclesia must be grounded in personal attachment to Jesus and his values: without the memory of Jesus the community makes itself master.

But the Church is more than memory, for it lives in the faith of the living Lord. It does more than look to the past for direction; it is a community of the Spirit of Jesus that faces the present and looks to the future. Without the Spirit, the community can be reduced to a group of museum attendants guarding a lifeless treasure. There can be an excess of memory: praising the past as the only authentic time, holding on to the past without being open to what the Spirit is doing in the present. We can lose the feel of the Spirit's presence now. When memory is embalmed, mission turns to dull obligation.

Not all the answers to the problems the community faces will be discovered by consulting the memory of Jesus, because Jesus does not leave behind him a comprehensive list of answers to every conceivable problem the community might face. The Spirit will be the community's guide as it journeys into the future and faces new questions. The future will be faced in the living power of the Spirit, not by an archaeological reconstruction of the past. When the community has a problem, they don't always say: "Jesus said this..." Rather, they will say: "It has been decided by the Spirit and by us" (Acts 15:29). Thus the Church has the ability to discover its future through facing honestly the new challenges it encounters in the power of God's Spirit.

It is good to recognize how much we owe to those who handed over to us the faith and the Gospel they loved, the people whom we remember as our own community of memory. The origin of the word *tradition* is "to hand over" not "to hold onto"—to pass on, not to keep. As time develops, however, we should become a community of memory for others; it becomes our turn to share the riches we have received. Like Paul when he described his ministry to the Christian community in Corinth: "I handed on to you as of first importance what I in turn had received" (1 Cor 3). Like Paul, we are the link between past and future, we are the community who have life in the name of Jesus and who are pledged to pass on that life to new peoples and generations, in the hope that they will learn to love what we love.

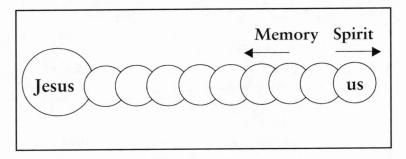

Luke has a vision of the Church as a community with two defining characteristics: it is linked to the past, and ultimately to Jesus, through memory; it is linked to the future through the dynamism of the Spirit. As John Shea comments:

Some contemporary thinkers have complemented this "line" image with the ambiguous metaphor of "contagion." The reality that Jesus unleashed into the world spreads like a disease. Each person who is exposed becomes, in turn, a carrier to other people. The revelation of Jesus Christ is catching. But this epidemic does not take place on the unthinking, bacteriological level. It is the result of human purpose and planning. Each generation of Christians, since the first, has preserved the memory of Jesus and, as best they could, lived within, acted out of, and passed on his Spirit. Tradition is a premeditated act of fragile people not wanting to lose what they love.[6]

According to Luke's portrait, the Church has to be a community of memory and Spirit, keeping these two in creative tension. A strange image of the community of memory and Spirit might be the dinosaur, the huge prehistoric lizard that became extinct about sixty-five million years ago.[7] One theory notes that because most dinosaurs found it difficult to move around, because of their size, they had a communication system attached to the base of their spine that warned them what was behind. This theory gave birth to this anonymous tale:

> Behold the mighty dinosaur,
> Famous in prehistoric lore
> Not only for his power and strength
> But also for his intellectual length.
>
> You will observe by these remains
> The creature had two sets of brains:
> The one in his head, the usual place,
> The other at his spinal base.
>
> Thus he could reason *a priori*
> And also *a posteriori*.
> No problem bothered him a bit;
> He made both head and tail of it.
>
> If something slipped his forward mind
> 'Twas rescued by the one behind.
> And if in error he was caught,
> He had a saving afterthought.
>
> Thus he could think without congestion
> And see two sides of every question.
> O gaze upon this wondrous beast,
> Extinct ten million years at least.

According to Luke, the community of faith must have eyes for what is ahead of it—attending to the new questions and challenges facing the community—and also eyes for where it has come from—staying in conversation with the tradition that has formed the community and which is rooted, in turn, in the Jesus tradition. Saint Bernard made the same point when he spoke of the Church as *"ecclesia ante et retro occulata"*—the Church that must have eyes for what is ahead and for what is past. The Church preaches the Gospel to the world it is sent to, and keeps alive the sacred memory of the one who initiated this life, Jesus of Nazareth.

The Same Spirit

There will always be a measure of conflict in the Church between those who instinctively look to tradition and the past (memory) to solve new problems and those who are more inclined to focus on the prayerful consensus within the community (Spirit) to find answers. This tension is evident at most meetings, whether they be ecumenical councils in Rome or provincial gatherings or local parish councils; people are soon divided into separate lobbies or camps perceived as traditionalist or liberal. They eye members of the opposite group suspiciously, distrusting the other's insights or arguments, confirmed in their own restricted viewpoint.

The truth is, of course, that both these groups need each other, for the Church is not a community of memory or a community of Spirit, but a community of memory *and* Spirit. Both characteristics are essential marks of the ongoing life of the Church, to stay loyal to its roots in Jesus and alive to the new challenges that face the community.

It is a mark of the writing in Acts that the activities of the Spirit are outgoing: the Spirit impels and directs preachers to new regions (Acts 8:29; 16:6) and equips the preachers in their task of evangelism (Acts 4:8; 6:5; 13:9). The risen Lord's gift of the Spirit is the missionary dynamic of the new community, leading the community to work they had not planned themselves. The Spirit that fired the first apostles and which inspired Saint Paul is the same Spirit which fires and enthuses the community today. Although speaking about the Spirit in the Fourth Gospel, what James Dunn writes works well for Luke's vision of the Spirit:

> The lengthening time gap between John and the historical Jesus, and the continuing delay of the parousia do not mean a steadily increasing distance between each generation of Christians and the Christ. On the contrary, each generation is as close to Jesus as the last—and the first—because the Paraclete is the immediate link between Jesus and his disciples in every generation. That is to say, the link and the continuity is provided not by sacraments or offices or human figures, but by the Spirit. The vitality of Christian experience does not cease because the historical Jesus has faded into the past and the coming of Jesus has faded into the future; it retains its vitality because the Spirit is at work here and now as the other Paraclete.[8]

The Spirit is the living force of the Christian life, the power that connects the community to the purposes of God. The Spirit works through us in our own halting attempts to work at peace and forgiveness and love. That is the language of the Spirit. Peace, forgiveness, and love form a language that everyone understands and longs to hear. It is the language that so many trapped people are literally dying to hear as they face death and loss and defeat every day. But who speaks this language anymore? Is it becoming a lost language?

It is the language that we, the followers of Jesus, are asked to learn again, to speak again. And when we speak it, the good news is that people will recognize we are speaking a deep language that is within them. It is deep calling to deep. It is a language that has no boundaries, and no special dictionaries are needed to understand it. It is the language of the Spirit in each of us. It is the only language that can call us out of hell.

Chapter Eight

Waiting and Anxiety

Reflecting on Ourselves

The impulse to reflect on our own humanity arises not just out of intellectual curiosity about human nature but from personal involvement, a healthy compulsion to find some kind of meaning to who we are amid the problems and contradictions that confront us. In self-reflection we cannot remain detached from the object of our thinking, since we are our own study; we cannot be indifferent about our conclusions since, rightly or wrongly, they are interpretations rising from our own self-understanding. We can, however, accept them or reject them. Although some people remain an obscure text to themselves, I think that most of us, if only for brief periodic moments, do pause to reflect on who we are and where we are going in our lives. As Carl Jung noted:

> One *must* occupy oneself with oneself; otherwise one does not grow, otherwise one can never develop. One must plant a garden and give it increasing attention and care if one wants vegetables; otherwise only weeds flourish....Meditation on one's own being is an absolutely legitimate, even necessary activity if one strives after a real alteration and improvement of the situation.[1]

Self-reflection is often counterbalanced by a critical sense of who we might be and what we could be doing. Questioning our own behavior is an essential quality of being human, just as complacency and the stubborn refusal to examine what we actually do and how that affects other people can lead us to become totally heartless. When we envision what humanity should or could be, we become naturally critical of what we are, as if we are gifted with some intuitive sense of what humanity ought to be. Unsurprisingly, the gulf that opens up before us can lead to feelings of anxiety.

There is a wide variety of disciplines that explore various aspects of the human condition—anthropology, psychology, medicine, sociology, political science, and so on—yet all these disciplines naturally tend to look at human beings from their own particular area of speciality. Traditionally, it has been the role of philosophy to examine what constitutes human existence and what is characteristic of being human. The distinguished Jewish philosopher, Abraham Heschel, set out to reflect on these questions in a series of lectures at Stanford University in 1963. In his opening lecture he noted:

> One cannot study the condition of man without being touched by the plight of man. Though biologically intact, man is essentially afflicted with a sense of helplessness, discontent, inferiority, fear. Outwardly Homo sapiens may pretend to be satisfied and strong; inwardly he is poor, needy, vulnerable, always on the verge of misery, prone to suffer mentally and physically. Scratch his skin and you come upon bereavement, affliction, uncertainty, fear, and pain. Disparity between his appearance and reality is a condition of social integration. Suppressions are the price he pays for being accepted into society. Adjustment involves assenting to odd auspices, concessions of conscience, inevitable hypocrisies. It is, indeed, often "a life of quiet desperation." [2]

I find this reflection refreshing rather than depressing; it is descriptive rather than prescriptive; it understands being in terms of living rather than vice versa. Heschel seeks to name what many people are committed to concealing, the reality of how we experience being human; he takes into account the surprise at what is disclosed in our living of humanity; he identifies the compulsion at the heart of so much of our lives, in pretending that everything is fine. He also recognizes fear to be at the heart of the human condition.

For some strange reason, many people are reluctant to admit to their fears and anxieties, as if these feelings are so rare in the human household that they have to be hidden: if acknowledged, people might withdraw from us and our immediate relatives might well feel obliged to refer us to a mental institution. Many people have an inarticulate awareness that somehow they are not matching up to the standards of adequacy set by society: they do not feel strong and confident, attractive and powerful, independent and financially secure. They become aware that the world they inhabit, as opposed to that of "normal" people, is full of feelings of self-doubt, anxiety, helplessness, and inadequacy. Rather than question the myth of the normal, most people disguise their despair behind a pose and join the ranks of the unreal, protesting that everything is fine, really. This adjustment, as Heschel points out, involves inevitable hypocrisy.

The Age of Anxiety

In 1947, W. H. Auden published his lengthy poem, *The Age of Anxiety*, which won him the Pulitzer Prize for poetry the following year. Although the poem is set in time of war, the cause of the anxiety is deeper than the occasion of war. The four characters share some common characteristics: they suffer from loneliness, feeling unattached to anyone; they have a sense that they are not of any value to anyone; they feel neither touched by love nor capable of offering it to others. Behind all their clever talk and apparent civility, the four of them live fearful lives.

> The fears we know
> Are of not knowing. It is getting late.
> Shall we ever be asked for? Are we simply
> Not wanted at all?

> ...this stupid world where
> Gadgets are gods and we go on talking,
> Many about much, but remain alone,
> Alive but alone, belonging—where?—
> Unattached as tumbleweed...

> Our subject has changed.
> He looks far from well; he has fattened on
> His public perch; takes pills for vigour
> And sound sleep, and sees in his mirror
> The jawing genius of a jackass age,
> A rich bore...

> He pines for some
> Nameless Eden where he never was
> But where in his wishes once again
> On hallowed acres, without a stitch
> Of achievement on, the children play
> Nor care how comely they couldn't be
> Since they needn't know they're not happy.[3]

The four characters have lost any sense of faith in themselves and any faith they ever had in their fellow humans. The scene takes place in a bar, and the characters, intoxicated with alcohol, seem to communicate not so much with one another—one character talks to a mirror—but through a series of competing monologues addressed to an imaginary audience, delighting in their ability to depict the panorama of meaninglessness that they perceive while refusing to take responsibility for changing anything. It is the conversation of hell, where people deny hope but refuse to call their situation hopeless, where people who are trapped forever in a wilderness go on, anyway, talking endlessly to decorate the emptiness with language. However accurate their ability to describe what is muddled and amiss with the world—the "clown's cosmos"—their insight does not lead to liberation.

While the characters are human beings, there is little that is humane about them: there is nothing that marks them as tender or magnanimous or forgiving. None of them seems to be rooted in a home; none of them is rooted in a community; none of them seems to relate to anyone. They are unloved isolated drifters, trapped by overwhelming self-disdain, cultivating self-disparagement as a virtue while defaming all around them. Nothing is sacred. They have no sense of themselves as worthy or dignified people; they project their worthlessness onto everything they see, contaminating everything they set their sights on with their diseased outlook. Their lives are anxiety-ridden. For them, the future is an unforgiving abyss. In the midst of war, you might expect these tortured and restless minds to agree with Shakespeare's Macbeth:

> Better be with the dead,
> Whom we, to gain our peace, have sent to peace,
> Than on the torture of the mind to lie
> In restless ecstasy.[4]

While you find yourself agreeing with some of the characters' observations, even envying their ability to articulate their angst so skillfully, you end up distancing yourself from these despairing voices and feeling revolted by the interior decay from which they must come. These four people are frightening, perhaps because their unrelieved anxiety writes in large and bold letters the felt anxieties we all experience. Still, you want to scream at them: "Get a life!"

Yet anxiety, admittedly in milder forms than the extreme form portrayed by Auden's four characters, is a universal phenomenon. It is usually experienced as a feeling of apprehension, a vague discomfiting feeling of uncertainty and helplessness. Mentalhealth professionals try to distinguish between fear and anxiety. Fear is a realistic response to a real threat, like feeling scared when we are diagnosed by a consultant and told we have a serious illness. Anxiety, on the other hand, is a feeling of apprehension about an unidentified threat: like panic disorders that involve severe attacks of torment, which seem to come out of nowhere, and lead to physical symptoms such as sweating, the sense of choking, and palpitations. In discussing this subject with my niece Susan Ferry, a clinical psychologist, she clarified the difference: "Fear tends to be a response to the physical self, while anxiety can be seen as a threat to one's sense of self. Panic disorder tends to have a specific trigger. Generalized anxiety disorder, on the other hand, is more free-floating and is often more distressing than panic disorder, given its continual presence."

In normal everyday language, however, people do not distinguish between fear and anxiety when they try to name their feelings of unease or disquiet. But what are these feelings connected to? What is the source of this unease and dread? Reflecting on her long experience in psychoanalytic practice, Frieda Fromm-Reichmann writes:

> I am primarily interested in demonstrating the ubiquitously implied acceptance of the concept that anxiety is connected with anticipated fear of punishment and disapproval, withdrawal of love, disruption of interpersonal relationships, isolation, or separation.
>
> This connection of anxiety as the expression of the anticipated loss of love and approval, or separation, social isolation, or disruption of one's interpersonal

relationships implies its close psychological affinity to loneliness. I believe that many of the emotional states to which psychiatrists refer to as anxiety actually are states of loneliness or fear of loneliness.[5]

In a similar vein to Fromm-Reichmann, the consultant psychiatrist and writer, John Bowlby, has consistently argued that the principal source of anxiety and distress is separation from loved figures, or the threat of separation.[6] Certainly, anxiety seems to be related to expectations of loss of love and approval— living in dread of being abandoned by our loved ones, apprehension about being utterly rejected by the people we respect, feelings of inferiority, fearing the disintegration of our personal relationships, feelings of isolation and loneliness, feeling scared about losing our essential values in life.

We can all add to this litany because all of us have shared something of these feelings of dread at some time in our lives. They are not alien to anyone's experience of struggling to live not just as a human being but struggling to discover what being human might mean. We all feel anxious at some times in our lives, and when there is no specified object, the anxiety can deepen, so we can end up in a circle of desperation feeling anxious about being anxious.

Waiting and Anxiety

At every Eucharist, after the assembly prays the Our Father, the priest prays to God on behalf of the whole community: "Protect us from all anxiety as we wait in joyful hope for the coming of our Savior, Jesus Christ." The priest petitions God to protect the assembly from anxiety, so that the community might wait in hope. Although it is entirely normal for everyone to feel anxious from time to time, acute anxiety can be a critical obstruction to waiting in hope; it can overwhelm the present moment with feelings of disquiet and apprehension, often with no specific object, making it impossible to wait in hope. As J. B. Metz noted:

> Patience is another quality that the anxiety-ridden cannot display. They cannot patiently cultivate those realities that require slow development and silent blossoming: love and fidelity, mutual understanding and friendship, marriage and family life. That is why these realities are in crisis today to a greater or lesser extent, riddled with an anxiety that cannot stand the slow place of deliberate tender care.[7]

Enduring love and friendship always require forbearance, long-suffering patience, to see the relationship through the stress of difficult times. Many people have no tolerance for "the slow pace of deliberate tender care"—afraid that life will pass them by with a distracted air while they are engaged in the endless round of attending, for instance, aged and sick parents. My sister Ellen looked after my father until he died at the age of ninety-four years, a long time of stubborn attention that was not free of anxiety, feelings that she shared with other members of our family. Although her care was enduring and gracious, she became aware of feeling anxious as the time of waiting grew longer and longer. For many caregivers, of course, anxiety is a normal characteristic of their attention to their sick charge; many, however, feel ashamed to admit it.

Professor David Smail in his masterly study of anxiety—*Illusion and Reality: the Meaning of Anxiety*—argues that feelings of anxiety are commonplace and quite normal in everyone's life, but in the ideal world in which we live there is little permission to talk about these feelings.

In the world of advertising, the "ideal" world that is communicated in images and language is indistinguishable from the "unreal" world. Advertising works on the principle that people are pliable and can be molded into any shape required. Many advertisements, especially those promoting bodily cleansing lotions or perfumes, appeal regularly to people's anxieties about their bodily features and their social acceptability. The formula is as predictable as it is asinine:

> Boy meets girl
> Boy notices girl has dreadful dandruff
> Boy is dismayed
> Boy rejects girl
>
> Girl seeks friends' advice
> Girl's friends recommend shampoo
> Girl washes with sponsor's product
> Girl becomes radiant
>
> Boy sees girl again
> Boy attracted by girl's radiance
> Boy strokes girl's glowing mane
> Boy loves girl

Most advertising is remorseless in its commitment to portray the unreal as normal. The aspirations held out to us by advertising confront people with images they cannot hope to achieve in real life: the happy family eating their cornflakes together on the balcony of a Venetian palazzo against the backdrop of the Grand Canal; unwrinkled middle-aged couples celebrating how their new washing machine delivers impeccably clean clothes to their hugely appreciative children; a young executive leaving the company of his peers to drive his real friend, a powerful sleek car, around empty medieval streets; beautiful young people with the latest cell phones basking in the admiration of their friends while making others envy their good fortune. Many people feel inadequate and become anxious because of their failure to achieve these ideals, believing they are so unlike what they are supposed to be.

In his study of anxiety, which is not dissimilar in thinking

to much of Heschel's study of humanity already quoted, David
Smail observes:

> For a variety of reasons, people are extremely reticent
> about revealing their worries and vulnerabilities to oth-
> ers, which reinforces a view of the social world, sub-
> scribed to wittingly or unwittingly by most of us, which
> is in fact much more a myth than an accurate picture of
> reality. Even more seriously, people are not simply care-
> ful to keep quiet about their personal fears—they are
> often unable even to see for themselves what they are.
> It is as if we have no proper language with which to
> understand and describe our feelings, but must rely on
> "symptoms" to give them some kind of communicable
> form.
>
> I do not believe that there can be anybody who has
> reached beyond the tenderest years without experienc-
> ing acute psychological pain over his or her feelings of
> inadequacy in relation to others, anxiety about his or
> her performance of socially expected functions and
> tasks, depression or despair at some kind of failure or
> loss....
>
> There are, however, quite a lot of people who claim
> to live lives unruffled by such shames and embarrass-
> ments, who make a show of adequacy which is to the
> envy of their friends....What may start out as a need to
> ward off anxiety by convincing others of one's own
> adequacy may end up as an ability to deceive oneself
> that one is totally invulnerable. Such invulnerability is,
> however, often bought at the cost of those who have to
> suffer the effect of the insensitivity and egotism that
> such self-deception needs to maintain itself.[8]

Most people's feelings of anxiety are a natural outcome of the
circumstances they are currently facing, an entirely reasonable

response to episodes in their life history. Feelings of fear or anxiety are not only normal but necessary for survival. To be wholly free of anxiety would be inhuman, a point illustrated by one of Grimm's fairytales—"The story of the youth who went forth to learn what fear was."[9] The story explores the bizarre adventure of a younger son, regarded as chronically stupid by everyone, who sensed he would always be incomplete as a human being until he learned how to be afraid. Leaving his father, who commands him to tell no one where he comes from or who his father is, he ventures forth and in a series of challenges puts himself in harm's way only to remain steadfastly unimpressed and unruffled.

Eventually he comes on a haunted castle, where evil spirits guard its great treasures; the king promises the hand of his daughter to any man who can free the castle from the evil spirits. Our hero survives all the trials and frees the castle. The king compliments him and says: "You have saved the castle, and shall marry my daughter." But the young man replies, "That is all very well, but still I do not know how to shudder!"

The wedding is celebrated; "but howsoever the young king loved his wife, and however happy he was, he still said always: 'If I could but shudder.'" His wife is angry and becomes determined to cure him. She discusses the matter with her maid, and the two women plot a way to ensure that this young man will experience fear. The wife follows the advice of her maid. When her husband is asleep in the marriage bed, she pours a bucket of cold water, full of prickly little fish, over him and he wakes up shuddering, overcome by fear. He also wakes up human: interestingly, he learns fear not from the dark or evil spirits or ghosts, but in natural surroundings, in the midst of a happy life, in the marriage bed!

The human challenge is learning to live with anxiety, accepting it as our subjective and often appropriate response to the ways we interact with people and our world, and to be free under its pressures. How do we do this as Christians?

Redeeming Our Story in a Larger Context

In the Christian tradition we are invited not to scrutinize our story in isolation—especially since feelings of isolation can be at the root of anxiety—but to place it within the larger context of the Jesus story, the one who paid the ultimate price for not fitting in to "normal" society. Jesus' insights and values, his nuanced interpretation of the Law, according to the religious leaders, led ordinary folk astray and made him deserving of death by crucifixion. From Gethsemane to Golgotha the story of anxiety is writ large for all to see: there is no pretence that everything is fine, no obscuring the pain, no disguising the sense of isolation, no posing behind masks, no hiding the real self. Gethsemane brings to the fore what so much of our society seeks to hide—the normalcy of anxiety and stress—providing images and a language that speaks powerfully and poetically to many people. As D. Soelle comments:

> From the modern perspective, Jesus' dignity lies precisely in his fear of death. A person without fear is deformed, despising himself too much to be able to have fear for himself. Fear is a sign that a person's roots are planted in life. You have to look out for a person without fear; he is capable of anything.[10]

In Gethsemane we watch an anxious Jesus, greatly distressed and troubled: "In his anguish he prayed more earnestly, and his sweat became like great drops of blood falling down on the ground" (Lk 22:44). He begs his friends to stay awake with him and begs God to release him; as the story develops the beggar Jesus appears to be abandoned by both, suffering the profound anxiety of separation. In the darkness we hear the terrifying silence, what Martin Buber called "the eclipse of God." In Golgotha the anxiety of separation becomes the anxiety of abandonment in the death cry of Jesus as he experiences abandonment by God: "My God, why have you deserted me?"

The Gospel story becomes a compelling source of teaching and liberation when we can connect our own fitfull lives to its narrative insights. Crossing over into the Jesus story and returning to our own can be not only insightful but also liberating. As Jürgen Moltmann has written:

> When we remember Christ's fear and anxiety, what he has already done with us and for us is repeated: he has endured the fear of being forsaken by God— the fear of separation; and he has opened up a way through this experience for those who trust and follow him. In fellowship with him we discover that we are released from anxiety as we endure it. By recognizing our anxiety in his, and by seeing it as abolished in his, we experience that "blessed" anxiety which kindles an unconquerable hope. To be released from fear means walking through the midst of fear, sustained by hope, because nothing "in the whole of creation will be able to separate us from the love of God in Christ Jesus our Lord."[11]

As the evangelists place the story of Jesus in the larger context of prophecy—in the belief that this larger biblical perspective will throw light on the immediacy of events in the Jesus story that might otherwise be puzzling—so Christians are invited to connect their individual story to the master story of Jesus himself. The belief is that the larger context provides a new field of interpretation to help us make sense of an opaque bewildering present. The answer to who we are and why we are the way we are now—as every counseling session presupposes—does not lie within our immediate context but in all our yesterdays.

The Christian thesis has an important addition: that the answer to who we are lies not only in all *our* yesterdays but in the broad narrative sweep of the Christian story, which makes the extraordinary claim: "Before the world was made, he chose us, chose us in Christ, to be holy and spotless, and to live through love in his presence" (Eph 3:4). The dream of God is part of who we are. We are not alone; we are not solitary archaeologists digging frantically among our own ruins, plowing for clues to discover why we have ended up the way we are. We have dreams to plow.

As followers of Jesus, we see the one we recognize as our Lord, suffering the anxiety of separation and loneliness, feeling utterly disconnected from those he loves; we even watch him enter the most isolated state of all, God-forsakenness, on the threshold of a violent death. Our anxiety does not separate us from him; paradoxically, it connects us to him, the one who loves us with an everlasting love. Our Christian creed proclaims that in Jesus' total abandonment and death, he dies "for us and for our salvation." If the source of anxiety is focused around separation anxiety and loneliness, the Christian proclamation can be understood to address that anxiety directly: we who are indeed unworthy are made worthy in the love of Christ.

The Courage to Go Beyond Anxiety

The theologian Paul Tillich addresses that deep sense of unworthiness in his reflections on anxiety. Tillich describes anxiety as a reaction to the threat of nonbeing, not only to the prospect of death and the fact that we do not know how this will happen but also to the fear of emptiness and meaninglessness. He writes:

> The anxiety of meaninglessness is the anxiety about the loss of ultimate concern, of a meaning which gives meaning to all meanings. This anxiety is aroused by the loss of a spiritual center, of an answer to the question of the meaning of existence.

The anxiety of emptiness is aroused by the threat of nonbeing to the special contents of the spiritual life. A belief breaks down: one feels frustrated about something which one has passionately affirmed, one is driven from devotion to one object to devotion to another and again on to another, because the meaning of each of them vanishes and the creative eros is transformed into indifference or aversion. Everything is tried and nothing satisfies. The contents of the tradition, however excellent, lose their power to give content *today*.[12]

Tillich's description, I think, is a perceptive observation of what many people have experienced in the loss of their faith. What was once treasured and affirmed is now relegated to the museum of one's former life: you can look at it with the eyes of a puzzled stranger, wondering how these relics once made such an important purchase on your life. Not unlike my atheist priest friend, in Chapter One, who keeps the ancient novenas he used to say to various saints to remind him of the world he once inhabited but has long since left: what once was precious is now the detritus of another age. And often there is nothing to fill the vacancy precisely because the radical loss of meaning is what has taken away the significance of these past religious treasures.

Tillich argues the Christian way forward out of crippling anxiety is the courage of confidence: the courage to have confidence in our existence, which can happen only when we have stopped basing that confidence in ourselves. This courage of confidence is not based on anything finite, not even on the Church, but solely on the ultimate source of the healing power in God, a God experienced in a personal encounter. He writes: "One could say that the courage to be is the courage to accept oneself as accepted in spite of being unacceptable....It is not the good and the wise and the pious who are entitled to accept acceptance but those who are lacking in all these qualities and are aware of being unacceptable."[13]

Embracing God and believing in our acceptance by God means participating in something that transcends the self; this is why the courage of confidence is needed. It is a decision that is made *in spite of* the anxieties and pessimism that might dominate our lives. It is precisely this act of going against the negativity we feel—this protest that leads us to move beyond the immediacy of the present— that demands the courage of confidence. For Tillich, of course, this is a natural consequence of believing in justification by faith rather than works: we cannot manage our own salvation but must rely on the merciful acceptance of God. Shakespeare's Portia makes the same point eloquently when she says:

> Though justice be thy plea, consider this—
> That in the course of justice none of us
> Should see salvation; we do pray for mercy,
> And that same prayer doth teach us all to render
> The deeds of mercy.[14]

Left to our own devices, "None of us should see salvation." We depend utterly, in the words of Zechariah's prayer, on knowing salvation through the forgiveness of sins by accepting "the loving-kindness of the heart of our God who visits us like the dawn from on high" (Lk 1:78). This is the courage to accept the gift of forgiveness in the encounter with God, as a patient might participate in the healing power of the doctor: no selfacceptance, Tillich argues, is possible if one is not accepted in a person-to-person relationship. This merciful acceptance by God is the only source that is able to take the anxiety of guilt and condemnation into itself. Only God, the ultimate healing power, can overcome the radical threat of nonbeing.

The virtue that enables us to confront and walk through the midst of our pain and anxiety is hope. We can face up to anxiety with the courage of hope, and while we will never be able to remove ourselves completely from feeling anxious—this would render us dangerously inhuman—we can learn about ourselves, understand what it is that is making us anxious, and walk the *via dolorosa* in the company of the one who is not only our brother but our redeemer.

Anxiety and Prayer

The simple act that sets the immediacy of our lives in the larger perspective of God is prayer, which moves us away from total self-preoccupation and places us in a conscious living relationship with God. Like all polite conversation, prayer begins by acknowledging the presence of the other: we are not devising monologues for our own consumption, like the Pharisee who prays to himself only to find that his prayer has reached its destination—himself (Lk 18:9–14). Prayer begins in recognition of the other's presence; it begins in polite tranquillity as we attend to the saving truth that we are not alone; it assumes the basic attitude before the other: "Be still and know that I am God" (Ps 46:10). In the stillness of prayer, we allow the God of all kindness to notice us, to come near to us, to attend to us, to listen to us. Clearing that mental space from the clutter of our immediate concerns, anchoring our prayer in the presence of God, is not only an important preface to all prayer but it can be the prayer itself: "God is not far from any of us, since it is in him that we live, and move, and exist" (Acts 17:28).

Faith is not just about believing in creeds and dogmas, but, more importantly, it is about *the kind of God* we believe in. Just as we adapt our conversation to the different types of people we meet, so we adapt our prayer to the kind of God we believe in. Perhaps that is why Jesus taught his disciples and us to pray to *Abba*, the one who is his Father and our Father. Jesus' prayer begins by placing us in the presence of God as his children, in celebrating the living relationship between God and ourselves. As the Catholic *Catechism* notes: "Thus the Lord's Prayer *reveals us to ourselves* at the same time that it reveals the Father to us."[15]

Our speaking to God may not be articulate and eloquent, like the flow of the Our Father; it may be inarticulate groaning, murmurs and grunts, cries from the heart that give expression to how we feel in the world we currently inhabit. In the great Jewish tradition of prayer, it is not only praise and thanksgiving that are promoted as prayer forms but also the wails of lamentation, the screams of brokenness, the halting cries of alarm and disquiet, the expressed fear that the one who once loved us will now withdraw the love: "Do not cast me off in the time of old age; do not forsake me when my strength is spent" (Ps 71:9). At the heart of this form of prayer is the belief that no matter what condition we are in, we should find some expression, however guttural, for our fear and anxiety. There is no human state that is alien to prayer.

Lamentations are cries from the heart, groans of anguish, screams for help, protests against what is happening in the midst of life. They are demands shouted from a bed of pain in the hope that God or someone will intervene. The protest at the heart of lamentation tries to free people from remaining mute and isolated in their pain. It aims at change. The first step out of speechless isolation is to find a language of protest. This movement refuses to stay with a "humility" that is indistinguishable from pessimism. Proactive behavior replaces reactive submission. Lamentation and protest build the bridge between powerlessness and change. The purpose of protest in prayer is not just selfexpression, but transformation; the protest is aimed at converting a painful situation into a peace-filled one.

There is no lovelier prayer than Psalm 139 in times of anxiety and stress, where the psalmist celebrates that everything we are and do is known to the Lord of all mercies:

O Lord, you search me and you know me,
you know my resting and my rising,
you discern my purpose from afar.
You mark when I walk or lie down,
all my ways lie open to you.

Before ever a word is on my tongue
you know it, O Lord, through and through.
Behind and before you besiege me,
your hand ever laid upon me.
Too wonderful for me this knowledge,
too high, beyond my reach.

O where can I go from your spirit,
or where can I flee from your face?
Behind and before you besiege me,
your hand ever laid upon me.
Too wonderful for me, this knowledge,
too high, beyond my reach.

If I take the wings of the dawn
and dwell at the sea's furthest end,
even there your hand would lead me,
your right hand would hold me fast.

If I say, "Let the darkness hide me
and the light around me be night,"
even darkness is not dark for you
and the night is as clear as the day...

O search me, God, and know my heart.
O test me and know my thoughts.
See that I follow not the wrong path
and lead me in the path of life eternal.
(Ps 139:1–12; 23–24)

At the other end of the spectrum is the prayer of contemplation, which Saint Teresa of Ávila defined informally: "Contemplative prayer in my opinion is nothing else than a sharing between friends; it means taking time frequently to be alone with him who we know loves us."[16] This prayer is exquisitely useless, fixed only on the Lord, wanting nothing, seeking nothing, demanding nothing. It is the prayer of the loving gaze, it is sheer attentiveness to the other—like two lovers utterly content to be present to each other without words. It is deep calling to deep from a place where language is superfluous. This prayer moves us away from the energetic expression of what is disturbing us to a deep silence within; I see it in terms of breathing out, emptying ourselves of all our concerns, while we breathe in only the breath of God. It is totally calming; it is being in the presence of the eternal attentive lover.

In an article in *New Scientist*, Professor Owen Flanagan reflects on the study of Buddhist practitioners that is being done by a number of neuroscientists. He writes:

> We now know that two main areas of the brain are implicated in emotions, mood and temperament. The amygdala—twin almond-shaped organs in the forebrain—and its adjacent structures are part of our quick triggering machinery that deals with fear, anxiety and surprise....The second area comprises the prefrontal lobes, recently evolved structures lying just behind the forehead. These have long been known to have a major role in foresight, planning and selfcontrol, but are crucially implicated in emotion, mood and temperament.
>
> With this in mind, a few prominent neuroscientists have begun to study the brains of Buddhists. The preliminary findings are tantalizing. Richard Davidson at the Laboratory for Affective Neuroscience at the University of Wisconsin at Madison has found that the left prefrontal lobes of experienced Buddhist practitioners

light up consistently (rather than just during meditation). This is significant, because persistent activity in the left prefrontal lobes of experienced Buddhist practitioners indicates positive emotions and good mood, whereas persistent activity in the right prefrontal lobe indicates negative activity.

We can now hypothesize with some confidence that those apparently happy, calm, Buddhist souls one regularly comes across in places such as Dharamsala—the Dalai Lama's home—really are happy.[17]

This group of neuroscientists are fascinated by the growing evidence from brain scans that Buddhist mindfulness in meditation promotes serenity and joy while at the same time seeming to tame the amygdala, the seat of fear and anxiety. Why is the "happiness center" consistently higher in Buddhists than in the rest of the population? Why is their calm and contented demeanor even more noticeable in our anxious age? This is leading some researchers to move away from automatically prescribing antidepressants to alleviate negative emotions to trying to develop meditation techniques as treatment for anxiety and depressive illnesses.

Who knows? While prayerful meditation will not free us from all anxiety, it might help us to develop the composure and serenity that comes from seeing everything in the larger frame of God's kind purposes.

Chapter Nine

Waiting in Joyful Hope

The Creative Word of God

From time to time we all bump into the awkward truth about ourselves that there is a gap between what we say and what we do, between what we profess to be and how we actually behave. Often we notice this inconsistency more easily in others. One of life's disappointments is to discover people who will promise you anything without holding themselves accountable for what they say. "No problem," they assure you. "Leave that to me, I'll do it!" And you know that the last judgment will have come and gone before they think again about their promise.

Sadly, the word of a few people is worthless. It's like Monopoly money—although bold and colorful, the wording is makebelieve and the notes have no real currency. But sometimes our own words are no bargains either: we lie, we draw back, we rework the truth, or we decorate the facts with so many disguises that the truth is lost under the weight of camouflage.

In sharp contrast to the fragility of the human word, the word of God is seen to be always effective because of who God is. As the Hebrew Scriptures note:

> God is no man that he should lie,
> no child of Adam to draw back.

It is not God's way to say and not to do,
to speak and not to fulfill (Num 23:19).

For God, to speak is the same thing as to do, to promise is the same thing as to fulfill. Genesis opens by celebrating the creative power of the divine word; God speaks the world into existence when he says, "Let there be...and there was...." As God's word made the first beginning, so it also makes new beginnings. Thus the prophet Isaiah celebrates the poetic majesty of God's word when he declares that as the rain waters the earth and makes all things grow, so the word of God never returns empty but accomplishes what it is sent to do (Isa 55:10–11). That belief in the dynamic vigor of God's word is what empowers people to wait.

One of the ways the evangelists show that Jesus speaks the word of God is by illustrating how he speaks with authority, unlike other religious leaders. So we see Jesus throughout the ministry speaking a dynamic word that is seen to be effective. In his healing ministry, for example, he speaks to people better—so much so that the centurion can send him a message: "Say *but the word* and my servant will be healed" (Lk 7:7). So much of Jesus' ministry is through his word: he calls; he teaches; he commands; he consoles; he confronts. When he speaks, something happens.

The Parable of the Seed (Mk 4:26–29) explores the power of the seed to grow by itself secretly; it develops unobserved in the earth and progresses independently of any human intervention. Even when the farmer is asleep, the seed sprouts and grows; the farmer is unaware of how this happens, but he knows that the seed's growth is not dependent on his attentive care. All he has to do is to wait patiently for the harvest.

But there is another parable—The Sower (Mk 4:1–9)— where a different dynamic is explored: this seed depends on the quality of the ground, just as some words depend on the quality of the response they provoke. The preached word is like a seed that is sown by Jesus, a seed that depends on the condition of the ground if it is to grow and yield a harvest. In the interpretation of the parable a variety of responses is explored through four types of hearers (Mk 4:13–20).

First, there is the hardhearted crowd who have no ground to grow anything: no matter what you do or say, it is never enough to penetrate their granite exterior. They have rid themselves of the habit of excitement; nothing animates them; nothing gets through. Whether you whisper love-poems to them in the moonlight or sing the music of the spheres, they will respond with an uncomprehending blank stare. Your words are left abandoned, like litter on the ground. Nothing gets through.

Second, there is the opposite crowd: the enthusiasts. These are the people who get excited about absolutely everything, who welcome every novelty that comes, who embrace every fashionable movement, who spend their life splashing about in the shallows. Sadly they have no depth to them. Nothing takes root in them, because they have no persistence or staying power.

Third, there are the legions of worriers. Although they hear the word, they are always somewhere else in their head, wrestling with their own tragic thinking, imagining the worst possible scenario. These people prefer their own catastrophic thinking to words of Good News. These people are disabled by their own anxiety.

Finally, there are the calm people who respect language, those who make space in their life to hear what words mean. These people welcome the word into their heart and make it their own, so that it becomes part of their being; when they speak, the new word is part of their story. The word becomes flesh in them. This last group of hearers are the model for true Christian discipleship: in giving the word of God a secure place in their heart, in making efforts to understand it, their willing collaboration ensures that this word becomes an event in the Christian life. Through their enduring support, they make words happen.

The parable focuses on the word of God that lives: in spite of all the obstacles around, in spite of all the wasted effort, the good news is that the seed does succeed in living and thriving and producing a rich harvest. The word of God preached by Jesus, despite apparent failure and repeated opposition, does reach great fruitfulness. The message of Jesus is heard and lived out; the word of God risked in so many unlikely places is indeed bearing fruit.

Waiting Inside the Creative Word of Promise

Perhaps the most defining feature of biblical waiting that we have outlined in previous chapters is that it is waiting inside God's creative word of promise. All the characters we have met— Abraham and Sarah, Zechariah and Elizabeth, Mary, Simeon and Anna, Jesus in the passion, the three groups that formed the core of the community of memory—are all waiting because they have invested themselves in the promises of God. From the different stories there emerges a unifying discernment that God's promise offers a new orientation toward the future, directing them to live in expectation, thus motivating their decision to wait and to endure. The promise itself establishes the firm ground for their waiting, offering an object for their hope.

Although the language of our own promises to others speaks in the idiom of "not yet," the language of the divine promise has a significant difference in that it speaks of "here but not yet." God's promise marks a new beginning and makes for new possibility. Something is inaugurated. Something new is already beginning in the word of assurance; a timetable, however vague or undefined, has been introduced. As Emily Dickinson observed about the power of the word in her poem:

A word is dead
When it is said,
Some say.
I say it just
Begins to live
That day.[1]

The word of God's promise has its own life, it possesses its own creative power for accomplishment, and it is offered as a pledge to be cherished and counted on until the time of waiting is over. The promise both initiates the period of waiting and makes the waiting worthwhile, giving it a sense of purpose. The divine promise makes for weighted expectancy. Like the psalmist who explains why he waits:

My soul is waiting for the Lord,
I count on his word (Ps 130:5).

Without the word to count on, without the timetable of promise, the waiting would be a fruitless exercise; it would be waiting in a vacuum, like the man we saw in the first chapter who waited in a snowdrift until he died, believing that God would intervene. Yet many people wait not inside a word of divine promise but inside their own wishful thinking. We have a neighbor in Hawkstone who is waiting to win the lottery, yet she never bothers even to fill in a lottery form and register her selected numbers. An otherwise sensible woman, she is stubbornly undaunted by the unreality of her wishful thinking as she cheerfully awaits the arrival of a check that will have numerals as long as a telephone number.

Wishful thinking can be an appealing pastime on dull days, but it involves dreaming without an accompanying sense of promise. Many people wish for things they do not have—the litany is specific as it is endless, including bigger houses, more powerful cars, more interesting holidays—but biblical waiting gives up wishing for what we think is best in exchange for trusting in God to deliver what is truly best.

The difference between what we desire for ourselves and what is best for us is illustrated strikingly in the following prayer found on a Confederate soldier during the Civil War:

> I asked God for power,
> that I might have authority over others.
> I was made humble,
> that I might respect others.
> I asked God for strength,
> that I might do great things.
> I was made weak,
> that I might do better things.
> I asked God for riches,
> that I might be happy.
> I was given little,
> that I might be wise.
> I asked God for greatness,
> that I might have the praise of men.
> I was given meekness,
> that I might feel the need of God.
> I asked God for all things,
> that I might enjoy life.
> I was given life,
> that I might enjoy all things.
> I got nothing I had asked for,
> but everything I had hoped for.
> Of all humanity, I am richly blessed.[2]

Waiting Together in a Community of Worship

We should not have to wait alone. As Paul Valéry, the French philosopher, noted wryly: "Alone you are always in bad company." He was not arguing against solitude or independence, only recognizing that we live by the strength of belonging to human community. Another philosopher, Abraham Heschel, makes the same point when he writes:

> Man alone is a conceit. Man in his being is derived from, attended by, and directed to the being of community. For man *to be* means *to be with* other human beings. His existence *is* coexistence. He can never attain fulfill-ment, or sense meaning, unless it is shared, unless it pertains to other human beings.[3]

This recognition of interdependence and solidarity can be seen very clearly from the origin of the Church. The question of *being* a follower of Jesus was regarded as inseparable from *how to be* a follower of Jesus. From the very beginning of the apos-tolic Church, people were invited not only to believe in Jesus as the Christ but also be baptized and join the community pledged to keep his memory alive and move in his spirit. There was a clear orientation toward community in the understanding that the best way to preserve the memory of Jesus was through shar-ing common worship and belonging to a fellowship of people who shared the same faith and hope. This is proclaimed in the First Letter of John:

> What we have seen and heard
> we are telling you
> so that you too may have fellowship with us
> as we have fellowship
> with the Father
> and with his Son Jesus Christ (1 Jn 1:3).

As the community of memory at the beginning of Acts gath-ered together in prayer, so the early Church developed rapidly through establishing communities which would do the same. Luke highlights the qualities that bind the early Christian community together in Jerusalem: "These remained faithful to the teaching of the apostles, to the fellowship, to the breaking of the bread and to the prayers" (Acts 2:42). While the portrait of the community is clearly cast in idealistic terms—"The faithful all lived together and owned everything in common" (Acts 2:44)—the stress is on their shared identity and kinship. After baptism the new members are not sent home but invited into companionship; they are not abandoned to their own devices but supported by the worshiping community.

That sense of belonging to a vibrant worshiping community, one that cares for the individual, is something that some people do experience in the Church and many more long to experience. A Catholic friend wrote to me recently to express her disappointment that when she stopped going to her large parish, after nine years of regular attendance, no one seemed to notice. She wrote:

> I suppose, if I am honest, I half-hoped that someone might wonder why I was no longer going to mass every Sunday and look me up to find out what was wrong. I was feeling a bit lost and down at the time. It was a bit humiliating to realize that I wasn't even missed, that my loss wasn't registered.
>
> I felt like the little girl playing hide-and-seek who runs up to the attic and hides, but then realizes after a while that she remains undiscovered—not because she is clever but because nobody is looking for her anymore. That's how I felt. Wasn't that lost sheep in that parable lucky to be missed and looked for and then, gosh, carried home?

My friend's experience is not exceptional as she waits alone. Having absented herself from the weekly worshiping community she now feels that the community has responded in kind by absenting themselves from her life. Her letter concludes by expressing the fond hope that Jesus' pastoral strategy—seeking out the lost because their loss matters to him—might also become the pastoral strategy of her parish.

In many places around the world, people are leaving large parishes and joining smaller communities where they hope to find a sense of real fellowship and a sense of their own worth; others are just leaving. There are, however, some success stories: for example, the Alpha courses, which attract young people and have now spread to ninety-six countries around the world; the growth of churches throughout Europe that are attended by immigrant communities— more than half of London's practicing Christians are now nonwhite. There is also an unexpected religious growth among young people. *Time* magazine's report on Christianity in Europe comments:

> Each year more than 100,000—90 percent under 30, and most of them European—pour into Taizé to spend a week meeting talking and attending thrice-daily worship. Many who come praise the peace of the place, says Brother Emile, who first visited when he was 17, and later joined the community for life. "People find life very complicated. They want to meet other people who are searching. They want to share their hopes and doubts."…
>
> As Europe has grown less religious, you'd expect that its youth would too, and in several countries— Britain, Spain and the Netherlands—they have. But overall "an increase in religion among youth is very clear," says French sociologist Yves Lambert. Among Danes, the number of 18-to-29-year-olds who professed belief in God leapt from 30 percent of youth in 1981 to 49 percent in 1999. In Italy the jump was from 75 percent to 87 percent. Even in France, which has Europe's highest proportion of atheists, the figure crept from 44 percent to 47 percent.[4]

Many people, not least the young, are searching for some kind of relationship in a community where they will experience a sense of belonging in a fractured world, a community where they can share their thoughts and doubts, a spiritual home where they feel they actually matter to others.

Relationship in community (what Luke calls he *koinonia*) is of the nature of the Christian movement: members are united with one another through their relationship with Jesus Christ. No one is a Christian alone: access to Jesus through the faith community. As Eugene La Verdiere notes about the members of the early Church: "Their common-union was made visible in their attitudes towards one another, in the way they treated one another in daily life and genuinely shared with one another."[5] The Eucharist both expresses and makes for that fundamental fellowship; without that fellowship the liturgy of the Eucharist ends up as pointless performance, belonging more to the theater of the absurd than to a church celebration.

The sociologist Robert Bellah argues that the habitual practice that tells us who we are as Christians is worship.[6] When we gather to take part in the shared eucharistic action, we are drawn into a network of relationships and connections; we are called to participate in a relationship of solidarity not only with the person of Jesus but with the people who make up the assembly. Bellah argues that this solidarity is an antidote to the radical individualism of Western society. The Eucharist is community-centered, not individualistic; it is inclusive, not separatist. Thus when there are barriers to *communio*, liturgy can be postponed until the members are first reconciled to one another: "If you are bringing your offering to the altar and there remember that your brother has something against you, leave your offering there before the altar, go and be reconciled with your brother first, and then come back and present your offering" (Mt 5:23–24).

The Christian community is pledged to come together in assembly and, in a spirit of reconciliation, celebrate the Eucharist in memory of Jesus. What we do in the assembly is a calculated act against forgetfulness as we follow the command of Jesus to celebrate the memory of his death until he comes again. The Eucharist is what the Christian community does while it waits; we remember and we wait together for his coming in glory. Yet the one we wait for is already present in the bread that is life and in the cup that is salvation, and we consume something of the fullness yet to come. The Eucharist is both a celebration of the Lord's presence and a recognition that we have to wait for the fullness of God.

If the Last Supper was Jesus' final act of fellowship with his disciples, it was also an anticipation of the messianic banquet that he would share with them in the coming of the kingdom. In the meantime the disciples are pledged to celebrate the meal not only in memory of Jesus but also in expectation of being reunited with him in the fullness of the kingdom. Memory provides the ground for hope as the community looks back and then looks forward to its future in God. Thus there is a sense in which the Christian community waits together inside the Eucharist, inside the worshiping assembly that looks forward to its own completion in the messianic banquet.

Hope and Help

Few of us in today's world need to go out and learn how to be afraid; many of us, however, need to learn or relearn how to hope. True hope does not depend on our shifting moods, on being in a good space, on being successful, on feeling exuberant about life and its prospects, even on being free of anxiety. As we quoted Vaclav Havel in the first chapter, "Hope is not essentially dependent on some particular observation of the world or estimate of the situation; it comes from elsewhere." Hope is a determined orientation of the spirit: as we saw with Abraham and Sarah, hope is not anchored in everyday experience but in a powerful word that comes from elsewhere, from the call and command of God.

This word comes to contradict hopelessness: it counters the outlook that some people share that nothing significant or fresh will ever happen in their lives; it refutes the tired view that we are all trapped in the web of fate, so we might as well endure it. The struggle between being realistic about life, without disguising the anxiety and pain, while stubbornly affirming hope, is explored in one of the most beautiful confessions in the entire biblical narrative. In the Book of Lamentations, especially in the third lamentation, the poet reflects on the interior exhaustion of his people, following their mass deportation, and he readily recalls the pain of the past. The verses do not conceal the prolonged agony, and they alternate between lament and hope. But it is hope, a hope that comes from elsewhere, that predominates the writing when the poet focuses on the true God whose compassion is never exhausted.

> My soul is shut out from peace;
> I have forgotten happiness.
> And now I say, "My strength is gone,
> that hope which came from the Lord.
>
> Brooding on my anguish and affliction
> is gall and wormwood.
> My spirit ponders it continually and sinks within me.
> This is what I shall tell my heart,
> and so recover hope:
>
> the favors of the Lord are not all past,
> his kindnesses are not all exhausted;
> every morning they are renewed;
> great is his faithfulness.
> "My portion is the Lord," says my soul,
> "and so I will hope in him."
>
> The Lord is good to those who trust him,
> To the soul that searches for him.

> It is good to wait in silence
> for the Lord to save (Lam 3:17–26).

The poet, in a sense, has to *remember* to hope in the midst of the pressing disaster he and his people are facing; when he broods on his anguish and affliction, there is no reason to hope from what he sees around him. His hope has to come from elsewhere, from beyond his immediate experience, from his faith in God's inexhaustible kindness. Without that determined hope he could readily settle into despair. He recovers hope by speaking his credo to his heart and this credo provides a larger context of understanding for the present moment.

Hope is not an interior resource that needs nothing but itself; if hope exists within us, it is because we believe that there is help outside of us. Hope is not absolute. As William Lynch observes: "The fact is that hope is a relative idea. It is always relative to the idea of help. It seeks help. It depends. It looks to the outside world."[7] Hope is dedicated to imagining a way out or a way forward; it imagines the possible; it does not stay within the constrictions of the present moment. If people feel totally stuck in a situation, they can lose a sense of the possible and so have no energy to hope. They stare at the present, obsessed with the detail and clutter of failure, and lose belief in the possibility of getting anywhere precisely because they feel trapped in a structure of hopelessness. The poet in Lamentations moves away from the detritus of pain and loss by seeking the help of God, reminding himself what *kind of God* he believes in.

Imagination is an essential characteristic of hope; imagination allows us to go beyond the present moment and envisage change; it refuses to stay within the limitations of the here and now. William Lynch observes the movement when he writes:

> For one of the permanent meanings of imagination has been that it is the gift that envisions what cannot yet be seen, the gift that constantly proposes to itself that the

boundaries of the possible are wider than they seem. Imagination, if it is in prison and has tried every exit, does not panic or move into apathy but sits down to try to envision another way out. It is always slow to admit that all the facts are in, that all the doors have been tried, and that it is defeated. It is not so much that it has vision as that it is able to wait, to wait for the moment of vision which is not yet here, for a door that is not locked. It is not overcome by the absoluteness of the present moment."[8]

Hopelessness, on the other hand, does not go beyond the limits of what is presently happening because it does not believe in the possibility of help; it has no energy to imagine, unable to envisage anything that could be done to manage or improve the situation; it cannot think of anything worth planning or doing. Hence the rejoinder: "There's no point." Hopelessness is marked by nonparticipation and noninvolvement in life: the hopeless want to be left alone to decorate their tombs as they retreat into the absence of concern. And they want to contaminate everyone else with their futile outlook: "What's the point?" is the regular rhetorical question of hopelessness. You can hear this question posed in family, in religious community, in the wider church, and in political life—the tired expression of apathy and futility.

Those who hope wait inside their hope. Being able to wait is an act of protest against the tyranny of the instant. The present moment is not an absolute atomic reality. Waiting in hope deprives the painful present from being utterly preoccupying in its power because it finds a larger context of understanding and a bigger frame of reference. This extension of reality does not transcend the present but sets it in a more relative, more actual time frame. Thus, for example, Matthew and Luke are particularly adept in their narratives at extending the time frame of the Jesus story backwards through prophecy, to the times of the patriarchs, and, for Luke, farther back to the beginning of the human story in Adam. As the risen Jesus did on the road to Emmaus, the evangelists constantly invite us to understand the events of the Jesus story in the larger frame of prophecy and sacred history rather than becoming fixated by the present.

In our Christian tradition it is above all Christ's resurrection from the dead that offers us an enduring hope. Christ's resurrection and our rebirth belong together: "In his great mercy God has given us new birth by raising Jesus Christ from the dead" (1 Pet 1:3). In the resurrection we celebrate that life is stronger than death; that God's love outshines human violence; that the cycle of evil has been broken; that laughter in the tomb supersedes the cries at the cross.

It is not just that God raises Jesus from the dead into glory; he also raises, among other things, the values that Jesus shared, the hopes that he cherished, and the kind of people he preferred. This creative act of God makes for the beginning of the Church. Luke goes to great lengths at the end of his Gospel and the beginning of Acts to show us how the resurrection and the gift of the Spirit, these two together, form not only the community of memory and Spirit but the new Christian community of hope.

Waiting in Joyful Hope

As a Christian community we live in joyful hope because we believe that Christ is our future, a truth we express in the prayer at every Eucharist, "as we wait in joyful hope for the coming of our savior, Jesus Christ." As the resurrection is the foundation of our hope, so Christ's coming in glory is the final prospect of our hope. This belief in the Second Coming of Christ is rarely preached now in mainline Christian churches; it is as if it has been quietly but effectively suppressed and left to smaller Christian sects and charismatic groups to pray about and think on. Yet the returning Christ is the completion of our hope, offering a new future and a radical alternative to the way of the world in a kingdom of freedom. As J. Moltmann reflects:

If the Christian faith is essentially hope, then Christians too will realize that when the Lord comes he will ask them, "Did you hope for me? Did you go on hoping to the end? Did you keep hoping even when you nearly gave up? Did you fall away? Did you endure to the end?" His questions about our hope and remaining in hope are important—so important that our eternal salvation depends on the answer: he that endures to the end will be saved. In the hope that abides we abide too and do not pass away.[9]

The hope of being united fully with the God and Father of our Lord Jesus Christ is one that is founded in the belief that our true home is our true origin, in the heart of God; that our destiny is our beginning, resting in the love that first loved us. In the profound and poetic insight of Ephesians:

> Before the world was made, he chose us,
>   chose us in Christ,
> to be holy and spotless, and to live through love
>   in his presence,
> determining that we should become
> his adopted sons through Jesus Christ
>   for his own kind purposes....
> He has let us know the mystery of his purpose
> the hidden plan he so kindly made in Christ
>   from the beginning
> to act upon when the times had run their course
>   to the end:
> that he would bring everything together
>   under Christ as head,
> everything in the heavens and everything on earth
> (Eph 3:4–5, 9–10).

Christian hope is fixed on the horizon when everything in heaven and on earth are brought together under Christ. Anxiety sees the future as a threat to the present; hopelessness sees no future that is different from the endless mediocrity of the present. Christian hope sets itself in a much wider context of understanding, indeed one that is cosmic, and is not limited by the constraints of the present moment. That can be seen most clearly in the death of the martyr. Christian hope releases the martyr from the finality his torturers presume to inflict on him: while martyrs from Stephen onwards have puzzled their oppressors by focusing on what is indestructible, their oppressors see only what they *see*, the death of a tiresome individual.

This can be seen clearly in a collection of farewell letters written in the face of execution by men and women of the German resistance, *Dying We Live: The Final Messages and Records of Some Germans Who Defied Hitler*.[10] The letters are an extraordinary testament to the ability of so many Christians facing execution to stay focused on the large vista provided by their faith and hope. One example will suffice. Father Alfons Wachmann was arrested by the Gestapo in Zinnowitz on June 23, 1943, and executed in Brandenburg-Görden on February 21, 1944. His last letter, written to his sister Maria, has the same date.[11]

Dear Minka:

At three o'clock I am going to die. Now the hour has come that God in his eternal love has ordained for me. Scholz, that good man, has heard my confession and given me the viaticum. In one hour I shall pass into the glory of the living God. I have given myself over wholly, completely, and without reservation to God. In his hand I am sheltered.

Receive my heartfelt thanks for all the kind things you have done for me in life. Blessings on you for the love you have given me, and for the forbearance and

patience you have shown me. It is with particular feel-
ing that I beg your forgiveness for having caused you so
much suffering in these last eight months. I commend
you to the heart of Christ.

Do not lose courage. Trust in God. He has not for-
saken me. The eight months of my preparation for eter-
nity have been difficult, yet very beautiful. Now I must
go home through the narrow gate of the guillotine. I
am convinced that Mother and Father are waiting for
me....

Dear Maria! May the almighty God, the Father, the
Son, and the Holy Ghost bless you.

UNTIL WE MEET IN HEAVEN,
ALFONS

From prison and execution Father Alfons sees himself going home: this enduring perspective of having a true home elsewhere allows him to move through his earlier anxiety and sense
of unending loneliness to picturing himself reunited with his
loving parents. Even though chained in prison, he chooses to
wait for that moment, a moment beyond his afternoon execution. Hope liberates him to go beyond the irrevocability of three
o'clock.

By choosing to wait in hope as Christians we give God's
future a chance to emerge. This makes our waiting both positive and creative: our waiting in hope is active because it does
not succumb to immediate anxiety or frustration; we can acknowledge and face anxiety and hopelessness realistically and
squarely because we remain fixed on our goals. Hope makes
you defiant in the face of obstacles.

Just as importantly, I think, we can also remain defiant of
success, refusing to allow passing success to seduce us in to placing our hope in ourselves.

There is a tiny passage in Luke's Gospel that tells of the
seventy-two disciples returning from their mission, overtly

rejoicing in its success (Lk 10:17–20). Jesus tells them: "Yet do not rejoice that the spirits submit to you; rejoice rather that your names are written in heaven." The disciples confuse achievement with ministry, celebrating that they were able to overcome the power of evil. What will they rely on when they experience failure, when their words are not effective, when they discover that what they offer is not what is wanted by people?

Jesus advises them to rejoice not in their immediate success but in an everlasting truth, that they are loved by God and held precious in his sight. Jesus leads them away from the immediacy of the present —in this case a successful mission, but that could easily change with circumstances—to focus on the ultimate ground of their identity, one that has nothing to do with success or failure: the everlasting truth that they are loved and cherished by God. In the language of Tillich, this is "the courage of confidence" that is not built on ourselves or on our performance but is founded in the belief that God loves us and accepts us.

Our hope as Christians is grounded in the truth of God's first love. Our hope fixes itself ultimately on the time when we can be reunited with the love that first loved us. In the meantime we wait. In the meantime we follow the advice: "Simply reverence the Lord Christ in your hearts, and always have your answer ready for people who ask you the reason for the hope that you all have" (1 Pet 3:15).

We return to a line of Roland Barthe's line that we quoted in Chapter One: "The lover's fatal identity is precisely: *I am the one who waits.*" Because we love and are loved, we wait patiently. As a Christian community we wait together in joyful hope for the fullness of eternal joy.

I would like to give the final word to Saint Alphonsus Liguori, the founder of the Redemptorists. Long before Barthe, Alphonsus wrote of the dynamic relationship between love and waiting, and expressed it often in the poetic language of living in a valley of tears while waiting and yearning for the everlasting joy of togetherness with the loved one. Alphonsus's ultimate perspective, whereby he saw humanity at home only in the fullness of God, inclined him to see human life in terms of exile: in the meantime, he wrote often, we struggle with our troubles and anxieties while waiting for joy eternal.

> Exile that I am in this valley of tears, I would that my affections were ever occupied in loving You, my God, but I am in continual combat with myself, whence I am weighed down and a trouble to myself....
>
> The royal prophet has said that You are ever near, that You endow with holy patience all those who are of sorrowful heart, suffering deep anguish within themselves. Remain beside me, beloved Savior, and give me the patience I need to overcome my torment.[12]

> This earth is for us
> a battlefield
> where we have to fight and endure....
> But when we reach heaven
> our state will be changed.
> There will be no more toil, but rest;
> no more anxiety, but security;
> no more sadness or weariness,
> but gladness and
> Joy Eternal.[13]

Epilogue

The Old Woman

O nce upon a time an old woman sat huddled at the back of a darkened sanctuary, waiting alone. A small flickering light, set in an ornate silver holder, accents the surrounding darkness; rather than giving out any light, the miniature flame seems like a lonely picket protesting uselessly against the supremacy of the dark. Only the rhythm of the woman's labored breathing and her mumbling prayers break the silence that pervades the cathedral. At times, it seems to her, that both the silence and the darkness have seeped out from this sacred space to fill the whole world; at other times she wonders if the darkness and silence have crept into this holy place from the pressing world outside. Whatever has happened, she tells herself, night seems to be everywhere.

She remembers the days, now gone forever, when everything seemed clearer somehow, when there seemed to be a collective clarity about right and wrong, good and evil, and those who exercised authority were regarded with respect. Now, conversely, it seems to her as if everyone is his or her own authority figure. Although not nostalgic for past times, she feels ill at ease in a world that is changing so rapidly; sometimes she feels ill-equipped to confront with candor its complex questions. These days, it has to be acknowledged, even she seems to have more questions than answers. Often she asks herself if this sanctuary is a sacred place or an asylum, a haven or a hideout. Is she here to witness to some arcane truth, to be a stubborn testimony to the enduring nobility of the Gospel? Or is she here to protect herself from a harsh world that seems to flourish outside the great oak doors of the cathedral?

She has been waiting here for a very long time. The days and months and years have slipped by without measure but not without incident, and she can no longer remember when she first came to be here. Nor, if the truth be told, does she always have a clear picture of who or what it is she is waiting to meet. Sometimes it seems to her as if the act of waiting itself is all that matters.

But somewhere deep within her own sanctuary she knows that there is more, much more, than this. Has to be, surely, she assures herself. She just has to think back and remember. Way back in the beginning there had been a reason, and the reason had been important. Someone was coming and she was supposed to be ready and waiting when that someone would arrive unannounced. But, if this were true, why was it taking so long? Over the years it seemed to her that she had been waiting endlessly: why is she still waiting?

Many times, especially when she feels bored, she reads the play, *Waiting for Godot*, written by the brilliant eccentric Irishman, Samuel Beckett: two weary tramps wait for a character that never shows up, so they pass the time as agreeably as they can by doing not much. She wonders, more often than she likes to admit to herself, if Beckett secretly borrowed her life story for his drama without a plot. How did he know that lives could be lived out like this, with people thinking of things to do while they wait, to give them the impression they existed? The first time she had read the play she had laughed and cried—the laughter of recognition and the tears of dismay. Now, she savors every word and scene, as if they were secret scripture.

Is she the third tramp? Is she waiting to join the other two onstage? Or is this sanctuary the stage for her solo performance? What is it that keeps her here long after she should have given up and gone home?

She keeps holy the memory that is deep inside her: she is waiting in this darkened sanctuary for God to come and repair a broken world. To stay here and hold fast to this hope seems a strange activity, for with every passing year the world seems to become a more fractured and more vulnerable place. New diseases appear and mutate into killer epidemics; new tyrants replace old ones in a predictable cycle of oppression; new ways of killing people are being researched and developed every month; language is being tortured as new phrases are devised to camouflage the brutality of innocents being killed. Caring for people and ideas seems to be regarded in so many places as a quaint medieval aberration that has, at long last, outlived its usefulness. The idea of progress—that the quality of life might gradually improve for all peoples—has been dumped in the rubbish bin with the beatitudes. Most people, especially the legion of the poor, have been abandoned to their own devices.

Sometimes people come and pray with her, and the darkness lifts momentarily and the silence is decorated with music and song. Her favorite composer, Mozart, comes alive again in this sacred space and she can almost hear the angels furtively draw closer to take notes. Sacred rites are performed, memory is hallowed, stories are told, and the Spirit, even if only for a brief moment, can be felt alive in the small community that gathers to break bread. Waiting together, she knows in her bones, is so much more hopeful than waiting alone. These moments of grace are becoming rarer, and she treasures them as signs to strengthen her dented faith.

Visitors from faraway places come to visit this cathedral that is famed for the delicate tracery that ribs the vaults of the nave and for the exquisite rose windows in the transepts. Periodically some of the visitors notice her huddled in the sanctuary: a few think she is an antique security guard and take photographs of her, for amusement's sake, while others ask her why she is waiting in the dark alone. What can she say? Sometimes she tells them the truth— that she is waiting for the coming of

God—and occasionally kind people wish her well. Now and then one or two people linger with her for awhile, though usually not for long, and then take their leave quietly, tiptoeing away to pick up the rhythm of their lives.

At other times, when she explains why she is there, a few visitors smile at her condescendingly—one person offered her the address of a reputable psychiatrist while another proposed a free session of reflexology—and then they return to the purpose of their visit, consulting their guidebooks and admiring the indescribable beauty of this ancient cathedral, all the time wondering why the place could not be used for some really useful purpose.

Occasionally she hesitates when she is questioned: she stutters and mumbles some inarticulate excuse, withdrawing to the safety of the sacristy and closing the door to hide her embarrassment and confusion. Waiting for God to come in power and glory seems such an old-fashioned idea; waiting, indeed, for anything seems old-fashioned in a society that thrives on instant access and instant delivery. A long time ago she had subscribed to the belief that God would come again in glory; more than that, she has invested her life in it; she has been waiting for what seems aeons.

Sometimes, however, the idea does not seem so old-fashioned but holds enough power to keep her waiting and hoping. She continually calls to mind her ancestors in the faith, especially the ancient steadfast figures, like Abraham and Sarah, Zechariah and Elizabeth, Simeon and Anna, all of whom spent a lifetime trusting in the promises of God and doggedly ignoring all the signs that might contradict their hope. Every day she prays to them, her forebears in waiting, for a small ration of their faith.

She doesn't always do such a good job of waiting. There are times when she grows discouraged and faint-hearted; there are times when she becomes distracted from caring; there are times when she wonders if God has grown weary of the earth and has created a new venture somewhere else. Why should God keep his appointment? Why should God take the trouble after all this time? When she feels like this she readily identifies with the words of the prophet Isaiah:

> There is no one who calls on your name,
> there is no one who attempts to take hold of you,
> for you have hidden your face from us
> and delivered us into the hands of our iniquity
> (Is 64:7).

There are other times, however, when her waiting is marked by faith and hope, when she remembers that God is always faithful and can be trusted until the end of time. She has always consoled herself with the biblical image that God is the potter and she is the clay, molded by the very hand of God. And she remembers that her waiting came as a direct charge from God. Had not Jesus himself told a story where he had said: "It is like a man going on a journey, when he leaves home and puts his servants in charge, each with his own work, and commands the doorkeeper to stay on watch"? (Mk 13:34). That means, she knows, that there is holy work to be done while she waits. Waiting is more than just sitting back and taking it easy until something happens. My call, she tells herself, is a command to active, hopeful waiting.

She knows that while she waits she has been able to help people: her very presence gives help to people's hope. People know where she is, they know she is there for them, and they have a sense that she will always be there. Being there is witness enough in a world where so many have absented themselves from being present to others; staying around and outlasting the comings and goings of fashions and movements, enduring the ordeals of her own frailty, all this must mean something of value.

Still, the waiting is often tedious and seems to stretch on and on interminably. Wars rage outside the door, hunger and hatred seem always to be gaining ground, and, for many people, sacred places like cathedrals and temples are a growing irrelevance on the landscape. Even when she is at her best, doing the holy work to which she has been called, the problems seem to outdistance her efforts to deal with them. What happens when the best you have to offer is not what is wanted by many? It certainly feels as if God has turned away, as if he is no longer concerned about what is happening to the world he is rumored to have made out of love. Still, there is nothing else to do but wait. Sometimes she hears herself whisper a prayer to ward off despair: "Come, Lord Jesus, come with power."

It is still quiet at the back of the darkened sanctuary where the old woman sits huddled and waiting. The sanctuary light is still flickering. The old woman watches and she serves and she prays. Sometimes she is both faithful and hopeful. Sometimes she is not. But still she waits.

The old woman's name is Church.

Notes

Chapter One

1. R. S. Thomas. *Collected Poems 1945–1990* (London: Phoenix Giant, 1996) p. 376.
2. "Where Did God Go? A Special Report on Christianity in Europe." *Time* (June 16, 2003) p. 26.
3. See D. Cozzens. *The Changing Face of Priesthood* (Collegeville, Minn.: Liturgical Press, 2000).
4. L. Appignanesi. *The Dead of Winter* (Toronto: McArthur, 1999) p. 97.
5. E. Schillebeeckx. *Christ: The Christian Experience in the Modern World* (London: SCM, 1980) pp. 37–38.
6. J. Gray. *Men Are From Mars, Women Are From Venus* (London: Harper Collins, 1993) p. 5.
7. E. Easwaran. *Original Goodness* (Petaluma, Calif.: Nilgiri Press, 1989) p. 13.
8. *Shropshire Star.* August 10, 2001, p. 25.
9. R. Barthes. *A Lover's Discourse* (London: Penguin Books, 1990) pp. 39–40.
10. G. M. Nelson. "Pre-Christian Peoples" in *An Advent Source Book*, ed. T. O'Gorman (Chicago: Liturgy Training Publication, 1988) pp. 141–142.

Chapter Two

1. *Time.* Cover story, "The Legacy of Abraham" (September 30, 2002) pp. 68–71.
2. V. Havel. *Disturbing the Peace* (New York: Vintage, 1991) p. 181.

3. *King Lear*. Act V, scene iii, 324–325.

4. S. Beckett. *Waiting for Godot* (New York: Grove Press, 1954) p. 7.

5. A. Rich. *Poems: Selected and New, 1950–1974* (New York: Norton, 1975) pp. 135–136.

6. W. Kerr. *Tragedy and Comedy* (New York: Simon & Schuster, 1967) pp. 19; 31.

Chapter Three

1. R. Williams. *Christ on Trial* (Grand Rapids: Zondervan, 2002) p. 50.

2. Quoted in R. McAfee Brown. *Persuade Us to Rejoice: The Liberating Power of Fiction* (Louisville: Westminster Press, 1992).

3. J. O' Donohue. *Conamara Blues* (London: Doubleday, 2000) p. 46.

4. J. Shea. *Starlight* (New York: Crossroad, 1993).

5. E. Gateley. *Psalms of a Laywoman* (Wisconsin: Sheed & Ward, 1999) p. 59.

Chapter Four

1. S. Monk Kidd. *When the Heart Waits* (New York: *Harper* SanFrancisco, 1992) p. 32.

2. *Macbeth*, Act IV, scene iii, 208.

3. B. Keenan. *An Evil Cradling* (London: Hutchinson, 1992) p. 262.

4. S. Weil. *Gravity and Grace* (New York: Putman, 1952) p. 170.

5. *Antony and Cleopatra*, Act III, scene xiii, 42–25.

6. D. Soelle. *Suffering* (Philadelphia: Fortress, 1975) pp. 36, 39.

7. W. H. Vanstone. *The Stature of Waiting* (London: DLT, 1982) pp. 29, 30, 31.

8. R. Williams. *Writing in the Dust* (London: Hodder & Stoughton, 2002) pp. 10, 11.

9. S. Heaney. *The Spirit Level* (London: Faber & Faber, 1996) p. 17.

10. O. Romero. *The Violence of Love* (San Francisco: Harper & Row, 1998) p. 152.

Chapter Five

1. J. Bowlby. *Loss: Sadness and Depression* (Middlesex, UK: Penguin, 1980) p. 245–24.
2. R. E. Brown. *The Gospel of John X111-XX1,* The Anchor Bible (New York: Doubleday, 1970) p. 931.
3. N. T. Wright. *The Resurrection of the Son of God* (London: SPCK, 2003) p. 712.
4. J. Fitzmyer. *The Gospel according to Luke X-XXIV,* The Anchor Bible (New York: Doubleday, 1985) p. 1587.

Chapter Six

1. H. Küng. *On Being a Christian* (New York: Doubleday, 1976) p. 76.
2. S. Weil. *Waiting for God,* trans. E. Craufurd (New York: Putman, 1951) p. 121.
3. E. Dickinson. *The Complete Poems,* ed. T. Johnson (London: Faber & Faber, 1975) p. 504.
4. W. Borchert. *The Man Outside* (London: Calder & Boyars, 1966) pp. 119–120.
5. C. S. Lewis. *A Grief Observed* (London: Faber & Faber, 1966) pp. 29, 30.
6. S. Weil. *Waiting for God,* p. 117f.
7. *Antony and Cleopatra,* Act IV, scene iv, 60–62, 66–68.
8. S. de Beauvoir. *A Very Easy Death* (New York: Warner, 1973).
9. John W. Lynch. *A Woman Wrapped in Silence* (New York: Paulist Press, 1968) pp. 271–273.

Chapter Seven

1. R. E. Brown. *A Risen Christ in Eastertime* (Collegeville, Minn.: Liturgical Press, 1991) p. 58.
2. E. Haenchen. *The Acts of the Apostles* (Oxford: Blackwell, 1971) p. 143.
3. L. Alexander. "Acts," *The Oxford Bible Commentary* (Oxford University Press, 2001) p. 1031.

4. For a fuller discussion of this, see D. McBride. *Emmaus: the Gracious Visit of God According to Luke* (Dublin: Dominican Publications, 2003) pp. 184–189.

5. R. E. Brown. *A Once-and-Coming Spirit at Pentecost* (Collegeville, Minn.: Liturgical Press, 1994) p. 12.

6. J. Shea. *An Experience Named Spirit* (Chicago: Thomas More, 1983) p. 20.

7. See J. Achenbach. "Dinosaurs: Cracking the Mystery of How They Lived," *National Geographic* (March 2003) pp. 1–33.

8. John S. Dunne. *Jesus and the Spirit* (Philadelphia: Westminster, 1975) p. 351.

Chapter Eight

1. C. S. Jung. "Depth Psychology and Self-Knowledge" in *The Collected Works of C. G Jung*, ed. H. Read *et al.* (London: Routledge & Kegan Paul, 1977) p. 817.

2. A. Heschel. *Who is Man?* (California: Stanford University Press, 1965) p. 15.

3. W. H. Auden. "The Age of Anxiety" in *Collected Longer Poems* (New York: Vintage, 1975) pp. 285; 287; 288.

4. *Macbeth*, Act III, scene ii, 19–22.

5. F. Fromm-Reichmann. "Psychiatric Aspects of Anxiety" in *Identity and Anxiety: Survival of the Person in Mass Society*, ed. M. Stein *et al.* (London: Collier-Macmillan, 1960) p. 132.

6. J. Bowlby. *Separation: Anxiety and Anger* (Harmondsworth: Penguin Books, 1978) especially pp. 101–181.

7. J. B. Metz. *The Advent of God* (New York: Newman Press, 1970) p. 27.

8. D. Smail. *Illusion and Reality: The Meaning of Anxiety* (London: Dent, 1984) pp. 13, 14.

9. *The Complete Grimm's Fairy Tales* (New York: Pantheon, 1972) pp. 29–39.

10. D. Soelle. *Suffering*, p. 80.

11. J. Moltmann. *Experiences of God* (London: SCM, 1980) p. 54.

12. P. Tillich. *The Courage To Be* (London: Collins, 1975) p. 55.

13. As above, pp. 160, 161.
14. *The Merchant of Venice*, Act IV, scene i, 193–196.
15. *Catechism of the Catholic Church*, no. 2783 (United States Catholic Conference/Libreria Editrice Vaticana, 1994) p. 667.
16. Saint Teresa of Jesus, *Collected Works of St Teresa of Avila*, trans. K. Kavanagh abd O. Rodriquez (Washington: Institute of Carmelite Studies, 1976) Vol. 1, p. 67.
17. O. Flanagan, "The Colour of Happiness," *New Scientist* Vol. 178 (May 2003) p.44. See also in the same issue, Dalai Lama, "On the luminosity of being," pp. 42–43.

Chapter Nine

1. E. Dickinson. *Collected Poems*, p. 534.
2. Quoted in R. McKnight. *Those Who Wait*, (Nashville: Gospel Advocate, 1989) pp. 28–29.
3. A. Heschel. *Who Is Man?* p. 45.
4. "Where Did God Go? A Special Report on Christianity in Europe." *Time* (June 16, 2003) p. 29.
5. E. La Verdiere. *The Eucharist in the New Testament and the Early Church* (Collegeville, Minn.: Liturgical Press, 1996) p. 103.
6. R. Bellah. "Religion and the Shape of National Culture," *America* (July 31, 1999) pp. 9–14.
7. William Lynch. *Images of Hope: Imagination As Healer of the Hopeless* (New York: Mentor-Omega, 1966) p. 23.
8. As above, p. 27.
9. J. Moltmann. *Experiences of God*, p. 36.
10. Edited by H. Gollwitzer, K. Kuhn, R. Schneider, trans. R. Kuhn (London: Collins, Fontana, 1958).
11. As above, pp. 111–112.
12. A. Liguori. *Ascetical Works*, Vol. II, ed. E. Grimm (Brooklyn: The Redemptorist Fathers, 1926) pp. 286–290 *passim.*
13. A. Liguori. *Joy Eternal: Devout Reflections*, Bi-centenary Edition, 1987 (New South Wales: Newey & Beath, 1987) p. 58.